CW01210861

Ransome Centre Stage

RANSOME CENTRE STAGE

2012 – The one that got away (see p.154)

Prologue

In the thirty years between the foundation of TARS and the Covid-19 lockdown of 2020, the society has presented a number of dramatic offerings for the entertainment of members. This collection is an attempt to make a more permanent record of some of the most notable. Many have been drawn directly from Ransome's own writings, though there are some notable flights of fancy which were well received by TARS members when performed.

Roger Wardale, one of the founders of TARS, taught at Nyewood Primary School in Bognor. His classroom bookshelf always carried "the twelve" and he encouraged his pupils to read them. There is no record of whether he put on plays before TARS, but in 1991 he started organising the 'Winter Gathering' for Southern Region members. Initially it was a regional AGM and some fairly sober entertainment, but it rapidly expanded to a full 'fun day out'. He brought his class to the Winter Gathering in 1997 to perform – for only the third time in history – *Aladdin* by AR himself, written for Withington Girls' School in 1928 (Ted Scott's daughter was there) and revived by Roger for his school performance, and then brought to TARS.

In May 1999, he presented that year's class in a *Trio* of play-readings of episodes from the books: the finding of the treasure (*Peter Duck*), Evellything Camblidge Fashion (*Missee Lee*) and The Legal Mind from *The Big Six*.

Sadly, there is no record of these performances, but

RANSOME CENTRE STAGE

Southern Region had already got their plays under way, as early as 1993 with the enthusiastic involvement of members such as Jill Goulder, then on the regional committee. We were split into small groups, who had to play key moments from the books, while the others had to guess which they were. My daughter Frances recalls 'skating' across the polished floor, and I remember being wheeled into the room on a tea trolley, with two small Tars and a penny whistle tucked into the lower shelf, while I, as the Dutch Pilot, was distracted by Captain John until I thumped on the upper shelf with a loud cry of "Now, Captain!" – and everybody guessed which scene we were doing.

In 1995, these meetings moved to nearer the centre of the region, at King Edward's School, Witley, and Jill introduced us to her new invention, "Amazon Dramatics": re-enactments of key moments from the books, to be recognised by the audience. There was also a Cream Bun Race, inspired by the episode with Bridget in *Secret Water*. Let Jill explain the rules:

Up to 8 Bridgets, and a Roger for each. The Rogers each have a bun on a paper plate, and the Bridgets clasp their hands behind their back; on the word Go, each Roger puts the bun firmly into their Bridget's mouth, and the Bridgets run to the other wall, touch it (yes, unclasping hands for the purpose but NOT touching the bun – we will be watching!) and get back to your Roger, who will rescue the bun and run to the organiser with it. Prize is for the fastest complete bun – teethmarks allowed, and a bit of cream loss, but missing bits or complete disassembly disqualify you. Bridgets who drop their bun will have to pick it up with their mouth!

For the organisers, she adds a cautious note:

Need buckets, water, cloths, paper towels.

The race was run, to everyone's enjoyment, alongside Jill's 'Dramatics' invention, which formed a major part of the Gathering, using what props came to hand.
We did this for two years, but the Dramatics were totally improvised, and there are no scripts recorded.

Meanwhile, in 1994 Brian Hopton entered the scene. He had founded a lively sub-group in the North Kent fringes of Southern Region, and was soon taken on board as a valuable addition to the Region's activities.

Brian Hopton and Tony Parslow on Waterloo Bridge.

RANSOME CENTRE STAGE

Southern Region

Brian Hopton

BRIAN HOPTON

First, let Jill introduce Brian:

Brian Hopton joined TARS in 1994, and soon became active in Southern Region, organising get-togethers and talks. He was welcomed on to Southern Region committee in 1998, where he served for 20 years. He and the late Tony Parslow became the indefatigable and imaginative organisers of entertainments for Southern Region's Winter gatherings, and for the TARS IAGM when it fell to Southern to host the event. The duo addressed with gusto every theme from pirates to Hullabaloos to the Russian revolution, with Tony as back-stage geek and Brian providing ideas, plans and the front-stage work.

This section, though, is devoted to an archive of Brian's plays and sketches, of which he was a prolific author, producer and director over the years. Tony was again the back-stage support, with Brian writing the scripts and dealing with the strange collection of temporary actors who responded to his call. The Hopton Irregulars came from all over Southern Region and ranged in age from 7 to 85: Alan Hakim, Paul Crisp (how could Col. Jolys or Capt. Flint be played by anyone else?), Peter Willis and family, Judith Powell, Brian and Diana Sparkes, Hilary Weston, the late Gilbert Satterthwaite, Aidan Musson, myself ... First came the letter in Brian's inimitable style (he never took to email), and then the phone-call with the full sales-pitch; we were drawn back time and again by Brian's enthusiasm, happy to support his vision and his devoted work in entertaining fellow-TARS. The performances were done with scripts (though actors were encouraged to familiarise themselves with cues and lines), but in full costume and with some set and props; a single rehearsal was carried out on the day.

One of Brian's most original and lively productions for Southern Region's Winter Gatherings was the *Sparkinson* series, in the format of the classic Michael Parkinson TV chat shows. 'Sparkinson' (Brian Sparkes, in a white tuxedo) interviewed a range of

RANSOME CENTRE STAGE

AR characters, notably Missee Lee. I was part of two, in 2004 and 2007.

Brian Hopton also used the sketch format, for example in 2001 staging five scenes (linked by a narrator) in the life of Ransome in his production *Inspirations* played at the TARS IAGM in Southampton.

But his first show, performed originally for Southern Region in 1998, was the one that he chose for his swan song on his retirement as impresario. *The Great Aunt Leaves – and Returns* is a short play telling the tale of the climax of *The Picts and Martyrs*, with Brian creating a series of brief scenes from Chapters 23-30, and it was played to a capacity audience at the 2019 TARS IAGM at Lyndhurst.

Brian has always been modest about his extensive contributions to the gaiety of TARS. He says 'Everyone gets a gift from The Almighty, and mine was a huge dollop of vivid imagination sprinkled with a fine dusting of rat cunning and perhaps an ability to see and use the skills and talents of others.' It's a fitting memorial to his terrific talents and energies that this archive has been created. Brian Hopton is beyond doubt a Certificated First Class TARS treasure, and we salute him.

In 1998, Brian was asked to produce something more exciting than we had had in the past. Here is how he described it recently:

It all began when I joined the Society in 1994. I read an article about getting together in groups of like minded members and by 1998, I had organised two lunches, a talk and an evening meal at our local cricket club. There I met great people; so much talent. We all became friends and I hesitate to pick anyone out as special but pick I must. David Towne and Gilbert Satterthwaite. They were delightful, funny and full of talent. David was a man of the cloth, Gilbert an astronomer, yet I was completely at ease in their company.

The talk I mention above was called "The January Sky" and I will address this later.

As most members will know, David, Tony Parslow and Gilbert have passed away leaving a great sadness amongst their many friends.

1998 was the year I met Tony; the year of our first play. I cannot remember why I thought of doing it, maybe on reading those chapters from *The Picts and the Martyrs* I saw the possibility of a play in them separately from the main theme. This was the start of twenty years on the Southern Region committee. Our main job became entertainment for the autumn gathering and AGM, which was the largest event of the year. The committee would decide on the theme for the day. This could be one of the books or another Ransome interest such as pirates, fishing, Russia or China. Tony and I would then think of some suitable ideas. Our aim was to attract at least fifty members; if not we took it as a personal failure. Here are a few examples:-

David Towne

Guddling, water divining, board games, treasure in a chest, fancy dress with prizes, real Russian prizes, a fan for every lady and for the juniors, dragons, chopstick challenges, loading dromedaries, also rides in a real rickshaw and always a super tea. Also for juniors, Arthur and Evgenia's escape from Russia with the help of a woodsman, the forest folk and ice yacht sailed by the ice queen across the frozen sea to England. Every now and then there was a ration of chocolate to keep the young Tars interested. When the theme was *Coot Club* and *Big Six*, Tony and I designed a game called "Getting the eggs back in the nest". Gilbert was P.C. Tedder complete with Norfolk accent and me as Old Bob of the *Come Along*. We were the judges. On one side was the Coot

Club and on the other side the "Hullabaloos", carefully selected for their horridness. Gilbert was very funny and everybody enjoyed it. Who won? Who do you think?

If anyone has taken on the task of producing a play, they would know the time and effort involved. Tony and I were lucky. We were blessed with a group of people who could act and write and wanted to achieve high standards.

Ideas and suggestions and a lot of the writing was done by Gill Gordon, Paul Crisp and Jill Goulder. So what did I do? Well now let's see. Tony did sound recordings, music, electrics, made props and worked off stage. My wife, Pauline, made costumes and alterations. My jobs were staying calm, telling actors how good they were and remembering hundreds of details.

The scripts in the following plays have been edited to include descriptions of the scenes that were not necessary when they were performed but to give the reader a better understanding of the plays. Some of the photographs were taken by the audience and others at rehearsals.

The only play filmed was the "GA Returns and Leaves" twice plus the mini-play "The Imaginary Muse".

Returning to "The January Sky". This was originally performed at the cricket club by Gilbert with a reading from "Winter Holiday" by David to "The Planets Suite" by Gustav Holst. There was a good audience including some members of Gilbert's Astronomical Society. "The January Sky" will always be my favourite show. The music of Holst, actually Gilbert's favourite music, well it had to be! David's reading of Dick looking up into the winter sky, feeling so small but triumphant and Gilbert inspired by his subject. But most of all the memory of my friends.

It was in this period that the dramatic version of "The Great Aunt Arrives and Leaves" first appeared. This was at the Southern Region Winter Gathering at Witley in 1998. As Brian says, we have a number of photos of it, which are used below. and there is also a very low quality video recording, which was used for reference when the play was revived at the 2019 Lyndhurst IAGM.

RANSOME CENTRE STAGE

The programme also survives:

TARS Southern Region AGM

WINTER Gathering

Saturday 14 November 1998
doors open 2.30 p.m.
Welcoming glass of grog from 2 p.m.
Finish c. 6 p.m.

at King Edward's School
Witley, Surrey

The Great Aunt Returns, and Leaves

A new play by Gill Gordon, from an idea by Brian Hopton, based on part of *The Picts and the Martyrs* by Arthur Ransome and produced by Brian Hopton.

The Play
Scene 1   A Fellside above Beckfoot
Scene 2   The Garden at Beckfoot
Scene 3   The Scullery at Beckfoot
Scene 4   A Ridge Overlooking Beckfoot
Scene 5   The Lawn at Beckfoot
Scene 6   A Tranquil Beckfoot Lawn Some Time Later

The Characters
The Hunters : The Audience
Colonel Jolys : Paul Crisp
"Cooky" – Mrs Braithwaite : Gill Gordon
Nancy Blackett : Jill Goulder
Dick Callum : Katie Handasyde Dick
Timothy Stedding : Aidan Musson
Billy/Sammy Lewthwaite : Gilbert Satterthwaite
Great Aunt : Diana Sparkes
The Doctor : David Towne
Jacky Warriner : Sam Waldrop
Peggy Blackett : Eleanor Willis
Dorothea Callum : Paula Willis
The Sergeant : Peter Willis

By permission of
The Arthur Ransome Estate

INSPIRATIONS

Three years later, Southern Region's turn came to host the IAGM, in Southampton University in July 2001. We naturally turned to Brian again:

When I first wrote the script for the play, I sent it to a leading member of the Society asking what they thought of it. Time passed and nothing happened. Then I met and stood next to that leading member at a 'Blackett' day. Nothing was said about the play at all and I guessed why. Then I had a phone call from a very embarrassed Dave Sewart, basically saying the play was not good enough and someone would send me a script. Dave and I were on good terms. I did not know what to say so did not say much at all. I was on the point of resigning from everything when two things happened to change my mind. One of the young girls phoned asking what clothes they would need for their scenes. She was so excited, I could not say it was all off. Then I received the scripts. One was based on the film *2001*. I politely wrote back pointing out that I was the writer, producer and director of the project plus the fact that I was paying for it.

At this point, it might be a good idea to say that none of the plays by Tony and myself ever cost the Society any money and all have the approval of the Arthur Ransome literary executors.

The second script was very different although far too long and sometimes off the point but I had some very good material in it. I thought some of this made it a much better play. I fitted the new parts into my original script and hey presto it was a finished piece. The name of that writer is recognised on the front page of the programme along with that of Jill Goulder who wrote and acted the part of the imaginary inspiration Enabler. Another good friend.

My wife could not believe I had so many good friends.

Unfortunately, the evening sun prevented any photographs being taken of the performance, but we have a few of the rehearsal.

RANSOME CENTRE STAGE

2001: A TARS Odyssey
INSPIRATIONS

INSPIRATIONS

Written and produced by
Brian Hopton

in collaboration with

Jill Goulder
and Paul Crisp

Saturday 30 June 2001
A SOUTHERN STARS
PRODUCTION

THE CAST
From left to right: Brian Sparkes (W.G. Collingwood, Arthur Ransome), Diana Sparkes (Evgenia Ransome), Hannah Green (Dora Collingwood, Lola Kinel), Jill Goulder (Inspiration), Heather Beal (Barbara Collingwood, Lola's twin, Josephine Russell), Judith Powell (Edith Collingwood, Dora Collingwood, Mrs Russell), Aidan Musson (Arthur Ransome) and Edward Bean (George Russell).

PROGRAMME NOTES
Do not applaud between scenes, sometimes these are only time lapses. Scenes in the play are imaginary and are only loosely based on known fact. The costs of this play have been privately funded.

© Brian Hopton 2001.
By kind permission of Arthur Ransome's Literary Executors and Josephine Russell.
Sounds, lighting and staging by Tony Parslow.
Programme designed by Joy Wotton.

Inspiration Jill Goulder

SCENE ONE: DEAD OR ALIVE
W.G. Collingwood — Brian Sparkes
Arthur Ransome — Aidan Musson

SCENE TWO: PICNIC ON PEEL ISLAND
Barbara Collingwood — Heather Beal
Arthur Ransome — Aidan Musson
Dora Collingwood Jun. — Hannah Green
Edith Collingwood — Judith Powell
Dora Collingwood — Judith Powell

SCENE THREE: CHESS BY CHANCE
Arthur Ransome — Aidan Musson
Lola Kinel — Hannah Green
Lola's twin — Heather Beal

SCENE FOUR: SLIPPERS
Evgenia Ransome — Diana Sparkes

SCENE FIVE: GOSH!
George Russell — Edward Bean
Josephine Russell — Heather Beal
Arthur Ransome — Brian Sparkes
Mrs Russell — Judith Powell
Evgenia Ransome — Diana Sparkes

Dedicated to all those children who have ever said:
"Gosh! I wish we had a boat."

INSPIRATIONS

is a group of five short plays depicting some of the people who may have been instrumental in helping the author Arthur Ransome towards the summit of his literary achievements – the Swallows and Amazons series, written for those aged eight to eighty.

WHO'S WHO?

Barbara Collingwood is the younger daughter of W.G. and Edith Collingwood. In summer 1904, her sister Dora spotted that "something was going on" between Ransome and Barbara: "She pretends not to care in the least, but I have my doubts!" Barbara married Oscar Gnosspelius, the original Squashy Hat.

Dora Collingwood is the eldest daughter of W.G. and Edith Collingwood. In 1904, Dora made a bet with Ransome: "I have made a bet with him, a cob pipe against a 2d indiarubber that he will come back next year." She married Ernest Altounyan and became the mother of the "Swallows".

Edith Collingwood is a portrait miniaturist married to W.G. Collingwood. She became Ransome's unofficial "aunt".

William G. Collingwood is an artist, author and biographer. He wrote *Thorstein of the Mere*, the story of a young Viking discovering Coniston Water, and John Ruskin's biography. Ransome and Collingwood first met at Coniston in 1903, and they became good friends.

Lola Kinel is a Polish girl who became friends with Ransome in 1916, when they met on a train as she and her twin sister were travelling home to Petrograd after a holiday in America. She writes about her friendship with the "extremely amusing" Ransome in her autobiography *Under Five Eagles: My Life in Russia, Poland, Austria, Germany and America, 1916-1936.*

Evgenia Ransome was Trotsky's secretary. She became Ransome's second wife in 1924.

Josephine and George Russell were at Levington Creek as Ransome sailed in one day in 1938 with *Cocky*. "They were waiting by the sluice as I brought the boat in and made themselves very useful. ... They became much valued allies. Both had a natural genius for small boats."

INSPIRATIONS

SCENE 1: Dead or alive?

[*LARK ASCENDING; SILHOUETTE as music starts; when violin starts, OUT FROM CURTAIN*]

Good evening! It's nice to be here tonight, and to see all you humans. I'm from the spirit side myself; I'm an Inspirational Enabler – one of quite a team of us – though for day-to-day purposes we just call ourselves Inspiration.

My duty as an Enabler is to inspire human beings like you; what we go among you to do is to help to expand the boundaries of human achievements. We can see what a human has within himself or herself if only they'd realise it, and we work to open their eyes to their own abilities and bring them out for the benefit of the rest of the world.

Some of my fellow-spirits have been responsible for really dramatic moments of inspiration, like Isaac Newton and his apple or James Watt and the steaming kettle. But I'm from the literary and artistic department, where we get some pretty tricky humans to deal with. If you knew what trouble my fellow-Enablers had with Mozart ... and looking after Shakespeare was a full-time job for a couple of colleagues too – though what a rewarding one!

For myself, I've had a few successes – Vaughan Williams, L.S.Lowry, T.S.Eliot – so I feel I can be pleased enough with my record. But one of my favourite cases – also a success in the end – was a long and difficult one; and I'd like to tell you about it tonight.

My work began high on a hill in the North of England.

[*AIDAN ENTERS*]

A young man wants to be a writer of poetry, and I've been given the task of helping him achieve something worthwhile for the human race. Fate has decreed that in fact he won't achieve this as a poet – but he doesn't know that yet; so I have to find a way of guiding him on the path that he must follow. Let me show you how it began....

Collingwood: Young man, are you asleep or perhaps dead?
Young man! Are you alive?
Young man! Are you alive or dead?

Ransome: Neither sir. I'm most fearfully sorry. I couldn't hear you above the sound of the waterfall. I was merely writing and taking advantage of this glorious day.

Collingwood: Well, I'm pleased about that. Would you mind if I rested here for a while and smoked a pipe?

Ransome: Not at all sir. I'd be glad of your company.

Collingwood: Do you smoke?

Ransome: Yes sir, I do.

INSPIRATIONS

Collingwood: My name's Collingwood, by the way.

Ransome: Ransome, sir: Arthur Michell Ransome.

Collingwood: Pleased to make your acquaintance, Ransome... If I may ask, what is it that you are writing?

Ransome: Trying to write poetry, sir, and rather failing.

Collingwood: Is it private, or may I see it?

Ransome: It's not very good...

Collingwood: I agree... but I also see a certain boyish enthusiasm and some promise. Do you hope to become a writer?

Ransome: It's my one ambition sir.

Collingwood: Ambitions speak of the future. What of the present? Are you at university?

Ransome: No sir. I work in London for a publishing house – the Unicorn Press.

Collingwood: Ah, a publisher, but failing to write poetry.

Ransome: Hardly even a publisher, more an office boy on 8/- a week. Still it keeps me in books.

Collingwood: Don't sound so melancholic; we all have to start somewhere. And is that one of your publications, the book in your pocket?

Ransome: This? No, it's a third of my travelling library.

Collingwood: Keats.... How apt.

Ransome: What sir?

Collingwood: A 'Pipe to the spirit ditties of no tone' ! It's from the Ode to May....Come, come, at least it's not from the 'Ode on Melancholy' !
What is the remaining two thirds of your library?

Ransome: Mayor's English Prosody and Hazlitt.

RANSOME CENTRE STAGE

Collingwood: Keats, Mayor and Hazlitt ... you are determined.

... Look here Ransome. I know what it's like to want to write. My family and I live on the other side of the lake, at Lanehead. Perhaps we may be able to help you with your writing. Why not come over, one day, and call?

Ransome: That's very kind of you sir. I'd be pleased to come.

Collingwood: Then that's settled. But now I must go ... Good day to you.

Ransome: And to you sir... eh may I just ask, did you become a writer?

Collingwood: Amongst other things.

Ransome: Collingwood! Collingwood! Not *Thorstein of the Mere*? But that was my favourite book as a child! It's a pleasure to meet you sir.

Collingwood: It's equally a pleasure for a writer to meet one of his readers, as no doubt you'll discover one day. Don't forget to come to tea one day.

Ransome: Oh I shall !

Collingwood: By the way, we've met before.

Ransome: Have we sir?

Collingwood: Yes, my wife and I shared a picnic with your parents on Peel Island ..... When was it, '95? No, '96.

Ransome: Goodbye, and thank you sir ... thank you very much.

****

Collingwood: That was ... oh, let me see ... 27 years ago.

INSPIRATIONS

How life has changed in that time. We were still very much Victorians; after all, the old Queen had only died two years before. Even Ransome was a product of his own caste.

The Great War was to change all that.

When I found Ransome sprawled on a rock, flying machines were figments of imagination for men such as Verne or Wells, and now the Empire air route could fly me to India in a few days.

Not that I'd want to. I don't travel much now ... too old, too frail. But I admit, it would be good to make one more journey ... to Aleppo, to see Dora and Ernest and the children. They were over last year for the summer.

Saw something of Ransome, called him 'Uncle Arthur' I believe.

Ernest bought a couple of dinghies and took them sailing on the lake.

People change as well. Ransome, himself. How shy he was then; and how tall and thin. Brown eyes. High cheek bones, and that red moustache, and now he's ... not so thin, and duodenal, and the moustache is more like that of a walrus, or so the children say. As for myself, the stroke was a confounded nuisance.

I've just written to him or rather, dictated a letter in answer to his:

RANSOME CENTRE STAGE

Thank you for your kind remembrance and message. As you can see I can't write and am doing nothing, like you, and therefore I am feeling better qualified to say ... I'm sorry for your troubles with the ulcer. But you'll get well soon, and I don't seem to mend. That I am still alive is the wonder, after all.

I'm most sorry for your continued illness, but I live in hopes of seeing you recovered. And perhaps the Blacketts and Walkers will do some more lively things; they are too good a crew to be dismissed in a hurry

When I arrived home that day, I told my wife, of whom I had met. She remembered that picnic on Peel Island with Professor and Mrs Ransome, and recalled, too, that he had died a year or so afterwards. Careless of me to have forgotten. Ought to have said something when I spoke of the picnic.

Well, my wife quite looked forward to meeting young Ransome, and my daughters were intrigued. Said we ought to have another picnic. But he didn't come, not until the very last day of his holiday. He was bound back to London. My wife was disappointed and the girls distinctly unimpressed. They had to wait a full year, until he came again.

Yes, it would be nice to make one more journey ... before the last. Aleppo to see the children, perhaps by way of Venice and Ruskin...

INSPIRATIONS

SCENE 2: Picnic on Peel island

So now our aspiring writer of poetry is on his way. He tries and tries, and he attains some highs and some lows – but he is no poet. He will reach and unlock his genius, but after a long and difficult journey of experience.

After the scene that we've witnessed, he went to tea with the Collingwoods and they welcomed him into the circle. They were an artistically-gifted family, and the environment allowed his own artistic spirit to flourish. There were three daughters in the family, and of course our young man fell in love with the elder two girls one after the other.

As well as being talented and attractive, these girls were spirited and full of derring-do.

Their house stood on the shores of a lake, which was an ideal arena for activities and adventures. They all went swimming there, and the family taught him to sail the little dinghy that belonged to the house.

Down towards the southern end of the lake was a small island; if you looked out at it from the shore below the house, it seemed to sit on the silver water like an enticing little green cushion.

On warm summer days the young man and the Collingwoods would sail or row to the island. Talking and laughing, they would set a leisurely pace in and out of the mass of little inlets and tree-lined rocky headlands along the lake shore.

[*AIDAN ETC ENTER*]

Once on the island, they would sketch or write and picnic, listening to the sound of the water and to the birds singing in their own solitary paradise ...

A YEAR LATER ON PEEL ISLAND. RANSOME AND BARBARA ARE SITTING BESIDE PICNIC HAMPER. DORA IS PICKING FLOWERS. MRS COLLINGWOOD IS

SKETCHING.
Barbara: Isn't it a beautiful day?
Ransome: M'mm
Barbara: Have you noticed how the water shimmers through the leaves and reflects back on them?
Ransome: M'mm
Barbara: Arthur, are you listening to me?
Ransome: Sorry?
Barbara: Oh really, Arthur!...What are you writing now?
Ransome: A poem.
Barbara: Upon what subject? No, let me guess.
Ransome: It's to you.
Dora: Just like the rest!

INSPIRATIONS

Barbara: What does it say?
Ransome: 'Shall I compare thee to a summer's day?'
Barbara: Shakespeare! ... You're cheating! Give me that paper. Arthur, this is rubbish! ... 'When I hear and talk to you, Life is like the first cuckoo.'
Ransome: But it's a poem from my heart.
Barbara: And now you're being melodramatic. Is that what *la vie bohème* does to you?...Dora, Dora! Come and rescue me from this silly young man.
Dora: I have a drawer full of these, most of them even sillier. I really don't think poetry is your strength, Arthur! ... Look here, how many articles have you had printed?
Ransome: Quite a number.
Dora: And how many books have you had published?
Ransome: Two.
Dora: That's impressive for someone of twenty ... And were either of those two, poems?
Ransome: No.
Dora: Then that suggests you are better at prose than poetry. Why not stick to what you have shown you're good at, rather than persevere at something you're not?
Ransome: Perhaps, or perhaps not.
Dora: Have you another book in mind?
Ransome: Actually yes. Have you met Gordon Bottomley over at Cartmel?... No?... He's a friend of mine. He's an idea of publishing a series of books of *belles lettres* and poetry by new authors. He's asked me to find the first few.
Dora: And do you have any in mind?
Ransome: Yes! Edward Thomas, Cecil Chesterton, and ... myself.

Dora: Oh Arthur, you're hopeless!
Mrs Collingwood: Don't take it too much to heart, Arthur, they're only teasing you. We can see that you have a gift for writing prose, but perhaps not for poetry. Keep trying and experimenting, and eventually it will come ... the right genre for you, whatever it may be.
Ransome: You're right ... I know you are ... And Barbara's right ... about those trees. The water does shimmer through the leaves.
Mrs Collingwood: That's the spirit; and don't forget to observe people, their character and the way they look and behave. File them all away in your mind's eye so that they're to hand when you need them.
Dora: Come on Arthur, stop mooning about ... it's too perfect a day ... Let's go sailing!

OLDER DORA ON HER OWN
Arthur and his poetry! I don't believe he wanted to be a poet ... just that he felt it was the convention to write poems as declarations of love. He really was a romantic, falling in love with almost every girl he met, and often proposing to them. I believe Mrs Ransome had to rescue him on more than one occasion. He proposed to my sister Barbara ... and to me. He was very immature ... naive in many ways, but touching as well. Poor Arthur ... I don't think either of us really contemplated marriage to him, but I have to admit that Barbara took a long time before declining, almost two years.
Back in that summer of 1904 there were too many other

things to do rather than become romantic. He loved being treated as part of the family, even doing the washing up or running errands. In the mornings everyone worked, my father writing in his study, my mother painting, and Arthur at those hopeless verses.

An Austrian cousin, Hilde was staying with us, and we three girls would paint or model with clay in a rather ruinous conservatory. Everyone called it the Mausoleum. But in the afternoons we would go off on excursions, sometimes for a picnic on the lake shore, where we would gather wood to make a fire for our smoke-blackened kettle. We'd eat bun-loaf spread with marmalade! On other days, it would be sailing ... voyages of adventure in a one-time fishing boat that was a monster to row, but not bad under sail. She was called ... *Swallow.*

SCENE 3: Chess by chance

Time has moved on, and our young man has matured somewhat, but his uncontrollable habit of proposing to each and every young lady that he happens to meet has led him into a most unsuitable marriage.

As a means of escape, he goes to Russia to work. As Fate will have it, this visit turns out to be of great significance. Working as a reporter for an English newspaper, he becomes one of a handful of Westerners to witness, first-hand, the Russian Revolution. During this time he makes plenty of new friends, and several of them help him on his literary journey. For example, his journalist colleagues teach him to write his despatches in proper telegraphese, and this helps to pare his style down into the clear, unflowery language that he uses when he finally finds his real literary voice.

I'm jumping ahead, though. For now, I'll just tell you about two of his

encounters in Russia, both with young ladies. The first encounter is fairly brief – but perhaps significant in planting the idea of a spirited young heroine into his subconscious for future use ...
[*GIRLS AND AIDAN ENTER*]
In November 1916, on a train to Petrograd, two young Polish ladies are playing chess to while away the journey. From time to time they notice a tall young man walking past their compartment. As he passes, he throws the occasional surreptitious glance in their direction. Then, suddenly, he is standing in the doorway, hat in hand and smiling broadly ...

CURTAIN OPENS.
IN THE CARRIAGE TWO YOUNG WOMEN ARE SITTING OPPOSITE EACH OTHER, CROUCHED OVER A TINY CHESS BOARD. RANSOME STOPS, REMOVES HIS HAT AND STANDS LOOKING IN, SMILING BROADLY.
Ransome: Please forgive me but I couldn't help but notice that you are playing Chess. This journey is driving me mad and Chess passes the time. May I watch?
Lola Kinel: Of course you may, come and sit, you can play one of us soon.
Lola's Twin: Here take my place, I can hardly play in any case.
Ransome: Thank you, I would like a game.
SHE MOVES AWAY, AR SITS OPPOSITE LK ... CURTAIN.
CURTAIN OPENS, AR SITS BACK SMILING, LK CLAPS HER HANDS.
Lola Kinel: Oh! You are far too good for me.
Ransome: Well I am older and have had a lot of practice. Let me introduce myself, my name is Ransome. Here is my card.

INSPIRATIONS

Lola Kinel: Artur Kirrilovich ... Arthur Ransome, you are English! Your Russian is so good, but I also speak English. We will talk in English from now on. I am Lola Kinel and this is my twin sister.
Ransome: You are twins! Perhaps I will call you 'Twin'.
Lola Kinel: And I will call you AK, as we are in Russia.
THEY ALL SHAKE HANDS.
Ransome: Are you going to Petrograd?
Lola Kinel: Yes I am looking for work.
Ransome: I am a Journalist, perhaps you can help me. I will give you my address. In the meantime perhaps another game?
CURTAIN CLOSES ... AS THEY SET UP THE BOARD.

RANSOME CENTRE STAGE

Lola Kinel SPEAKING TO AUDIENCE
After that train journey, we continued to meet, at first he used to call at our house, but I think he found our people 'bourgeois', though he was not quite so rude as to say so. He was very much a bohemian. One day I went to his room overlooking St. Isaac's Square, to deliver some books. It was the first bachelor room I had ever seen. He had a large room in an old boarding house. It had a desk and typewriter in one corner, in another a bed, night table and dresser, all behind a screen. Then there was a sort of social arrangement of an old sofa and a round table with some chairs around it in the centre. But the main thing was books ... everywhere! They were heaped in rows on the dresser, on the chairs, on the sofa and even on the floor.

CURTAIN OPENS ON RANSOME'S ROOM. HE IS AT HIS DESK. LOLA ENTERS WITH A PILE OF BOOKS. SHE PUTS THEM DOWN AND NOTICES A DISCARDED SOCK. SHE PICKS IT UP GINGERLY WITH A PIECE OF PAPER.
Lola Kinel: Doesn't anyone mend your socks for you?
Ransome: No! Don't bother with those, the maid forgets to pick them up and the Russian PRACHKI never mend anything.
Lola Kinel: You must buy an awful lot of socks.
Ransome: I do, I live like a wild rabbit.
Lola Kinel: And look at your desk ... all this dust, does the maid never clean?
Ransome: She dare not. I would wring her neck if she did.
Lola Kinel: You are like a child. How old are you?

INSPIRATIONS

Ransome: Thirty-four.
Lola Kinel: I am eighteen and have more sense.
Ransome: Eighteen! In England you would still be in the nursery. You are very sophisticated.
Lola Kinel: How old did you think I was. No lying!
Ransome: Oh! About twenty-three, twenty-five.
Lola Kinel: Really!
SHE PREENS HERSELF AND LOOKS PLEASED … CURTAIN CLOSES.

Lola Kinel SPEAKING TO AUDIENCE
It was in March the following year when the first revolution occurred, and there were skirmishes in the streets. This did not worry me. It was exciting! Ah, the impetuosity of youth! One fine sunny; day I met AK and we went toward the river, the snow crunching beneath our boots. We noticed a detachment of soldiers walking to the bridges. With a correspondent's nose for news AK decided to follow them. I almost had to run to keep up. Just as we approached the bridge, I saw a detachment of the other side also approaching the bridge. AK was excited. When they were about 200 paces apart they halted and the front rows knelt. Almost simultaneously, they opened fire.

CURTAIN OPENS: AR AND LOLA ARE WALKING IN THE STREET AND SEE SOLDIERS ON THE MARCH.
Ransome: There is going to be a fight here, I must watch. You take cover.
LOLA DOES NOT MOVE. THERE IS THE SOUND OF FIRING. THEY STAND TRANSFIXED. SUDDENLY:

RANSOME CENTRE STAGE

Ransome: Good God! I forgot you were here, Twin, come away.
Lola Kinel: No, No! I want to watch: I don't want to go.
Ransome: Come on, do you want to be killed?
AR PULLS HER TO THE SIDE OF THE STAGE. THEY STOP, PANTING.
Twin! Phew! I think we're safe here. You are either crazy, or the bravest girl I have ever met.
AR SHAKES HIS HEAD. LOLA SMILES UP AT HIM ... CURTAIN CLOSES.

Lola Kinel SPEAKING TO AUDIENCE
Have you ever heard bullets go past? They seem to whistle with a characteristic swishing sound. The crack of a report comes a second later. When AK realised that I was in danger, he half-dragged, half-carried me to safety round a corner away from the bullets. Only then did he put me down. It was very romantic. Many years later in the warmth of California, a long way from where those bullets flicked overhead and the snow crunched beneath our feet. I saw a book by AK for sale in a book shop. I bought it. It was called *Pigeon Post*. It was about children and I liked it very much, especially the characters of the children. My favourite was Nancy, so much spirit, she could almost have been a Russian, or a Pole!

INSPIRATIONS

SCENE 4: Slippers

So that was one of his encounters – with a fearless girl who might just fit into a book one day, perhaps ...?

His second encounter happened again during his adventurous and often dangerous time in Russia, and as a result of the meetings that he as a journalist had with the key men in the hierarchy of the revolutionaries.

In the office of Trotsky, Lenin's right-hand man, Ransome met his second young lady, 23-year-old Evgenia Petrovna Shelyepina. They were very much attracted to each other, and before long he realised that he wanted her by his side for good. He determined to bring her to England, and after a catalogue of adventures and risky moments he succeeded. She was brave and resourceful, and a suitable long-term mate for the maturing Ransome. Following his divorce, she became his wife.

In about 1928, Ransome comes to a crossroads. He has the choice of security with the newspaper for which he works – but this means effective imprisonment in its offices – or of living hand-to-mouth as a freelance writer, when he will be at liberty to fish in the rivers and sail on his beloved lakes.

Both fate and inspiration take a hand here, when the children of Dora Collingwood (one of his first loves) come to give him a present for his half-forgotten birthday. He is, in turn, annoyed at being interrupted, delighted at their gift and finally guilt-ridden by his initial bad-tempered thoughts. To redeem himself he decides to write the children a little story, which he dedicated 'To the six for whom it was written in exchange for a pair of slippers.'

Evgenia, not knowing how this event is to change their lives, has her own views on the new development. Even so, despite her grumbles, she will support him come what may.

CURTAIN OPENS
EVGENIA APPEARS AND CROSSES THE STAGE, PAUSES,

LOOKS AT THE SLIPPERS, SIGHS AND SHRUGS. DISAPPEARS INTO WINGS AND RE-APPEARS WITH A BOTTLE AND GLASS. SHE SITS DOWN AT THE TABLE, LOOKS AGAIN AT THE SLIPPERS, SIGHS AND LOOKS UP TO HEAVEN. SHE POURS A DRINK AND TAKES A SIP.
Slippers! For what does he need such slippers?
SHE SPREADS HER HANDS
Still the children were so happy to bring the gift and now he feels VERY guilty for being so short with them.
SHE TAKES ANOTHER DRINK
A little story he said, in a way of saying thank you. That was two weeks ago and his proper work not even finished yet.
His head is full of pirates and sailing. All the time he walks up and down, up and down, talking, chuckling and arguing with himself.
They've taken over! This 'Nancy' child won't do as she is told. HUH !
SHE FOLDS HER ARMS AND LOOKS FIERCE
That I would not tolerate from any child ... PIRATES indeed. Cape sends letters. Where are the Fishing Essays? Nowhere is where they are.
SHE TAKES ANOTHER DRINK.
Every night a pile of paper comes to bed with us. He places it by the bed so that he can touch it. I have seen him do it. Who would want to steal it is a mystery to me. This little story is becoming a BOOK.
I know he is unhappy working for the Newspaper. Ted Scott has offered him a permanent position, but Arthur is terrified of being trapped in what he calls a life sentence in

INSPIRATIONS

the CORRIDOR.
Still it is money coming in ... but all he wants to do is write a book or two between his sailing and fishing ... That is all very well but it does not pay the bills.
So! What is it to be ... a safe but unhappy existence ... or a gypsy life, waiting for a Publisher's cheque?
I do not know ... but he is so happy at the moment ... I won't go on about the Fishing Essays.
SHE HOLDS UP THE SLIPPERS AND PEERS AT THEM
Who knows? ... perhaps this is a turning point, I must be with him if he decides against the CORRIDOR.... so we will have to make a few sacrifices. Did we not make them in Russia?
We did not come all this way, through all those dangers...just to live in a CORRIDOR.
Perhaps he will write a nice book that will make enough money, so that we can live in a better place ... somewhere where it stops raining once in a while ... somewhere with a nice garden that has more than an inch of soil in it ... Somewhere where the shops are not eight miles away ... AND I have walked it.
SHE GETS UP, GOES TO THE WINGS AND LOOKS UP. THEN RETURNS TO THE TABLE AND TAKES ANOTHER DRINK
Soon I must make the supper, he will be down to say he has written only two pages, I can't think why it takes so long. It is only for children, after all ... then it is worry, worry, worry.
He will ask me what I think and I will tell him ... then he will be upset ... but I can't help that, I say what I feel ... it

is my nature.
Still! ... Let him finish his story and then I will mention the Essays again and then ...
SHE STANDS UP, PICKS UP THE BOTTLE AND GLASS AND WALKS TOWARDS THE WINGS, PAUSES AND LOOKS OUT OVER THE AUDIENCE
... we will have to start talking about CORRIDORS.
Arthur! Supper's ready.
CURTAINS CLOSE

SCENE 5: Gosh!
Well, that 'little story' did become a book, which was published and sold well, prompting our one-time poet and journalist to write further books of the same sort. Soon the Ransomes are financially secure, which is just as well as Arthur has been dogged by illness for some years.
The children who inspired the first book have grown; Ransome is feeling the need for a fresh crew of young children as models for his later books. In 1937 he and Evgenia move to the East Coast. Following a very successful book about that area, he has another story in mind and is on the lookout for some inspiration
[*CHILDREN ENTER, WATER NOISE*]
So here we have two youngsters, Josephine and George Russell, walking along the banks of the River Orwell. It's the school holidays, and they're rather bored ...

JOSEPHINE AND GEORGE RUSSELL ARE WALKING ALONG THE BANKS OF THE RIVER ORWELL. IT IS THE SCHOOL HOLIDAYS. THEY ARE RATHER BORED.
George: I say, I wish we had something more to do than just walk about all day long.
Josephine: Well mummy did say that we could go into

INSPIRATIONS

Ipswich one day.
GEORGE PICKS UP A STONE AND SKIMS IT ON TO WATER.
George: Not that sort of thing, I mean real adventure. Gosh! I wish we had a boat ... look at them, some of them are huge. I bet they can even go to sea.
Josephine: But we don't know how to sail and it would take ages to learn, even to sail a little one ... like that one coming down the river now.
George: Which one?
Josephine: There ... the one with the square, red sail.
George: Oh yes! ... I see it, let's watch and see how it's done.
Josephine: There is a very large man sailing it.
George: Sailing HER! ... I say, he's steering straight for this landing stage.
Josephine: He's waving and shouting something.
Ransome: Ahoy there ... can you catch a line for me and hold tight, while I get her alongside.
George: Gosh!
Josephine: You had better do it George.
Ransome: That's it, now make it fast while I bring down the sail ... That's the way ... Well done ...
Thanks very much, a bit tricky that, what with the tide ... So what are the names of my young rescuers?
George: I'm George Russell and this is my sister Josephine ... We live just over there.
Ransome: Well it would seem that we are nearly neighbours.
My wife and I are staying at Broke Farm ... I would not be

surprised if we meet again ... Oh! My name is Ransome, by the way ... Till we meet again then. Goodbye.
Josephine: You don't think it's him, do you?
George: Don't be stupid, there must be thousands of Ransomes ..... It's even on our lawnmower .
Josephine: Oh! well, it must be nearly teatime, let's go and tell Mummy.
THEY RUN OFF ... CURTAIN CLOSES.

CURTAIN OPENS. MRS RUSSELL IS KNITTING. GEORGE AND JOSEPHINE ENTER.
Mrs Russell: Hello dears, you're early for tea ... for a change.
Josephine: Mummy! we helped a man moor his boat, he lives at Broke Farm and his name is RANSOME.
George: She thinks he's the chap who wrote the books. Most unlikely I would have thought.
Mrs Russell: In fact Josephine is quite right, he is the chap who writes the books that you like so much. I have already met Mrs Ransome, a Russian lady. Very keen on gardening.
Josephine: Oh! Mother, if only we could meet him properly.
Mrs Russell: Well ... I have some plants that I promised her, perhaps if I invited them to tea one day?
Josephine: Oh! please Mummy, ask them tomorrow.
Mrs Russell: No promises mind, I'll see what I can do.
CURTAIN CLOSES.
CURTAIN OPENS. MRS RUSSELL, EVGENIA, ARTHUR, JOSEPHINE AND GEORGE ARE SITTING IN THE LOUNGE.

INSPIRATIONS

Evgenia: That was a very nice sponge cake Mrs Russell, you must give me the recipe.
Mrs Russell: Thank you Mrs Ransome, I will send it round to you.
Evgenia: Those plants you gave me are doing very well, mind you I'm not surprised, it never stops raining in this country.
Mrs Russell: Yes, our weather is rather predictable.
Ransome: Mrs Russell, I have been wondering if I might borrow these two. I have plans for a new book to be set on Hamford Water. It would help me to have some role models, sailing and camping, that sort of thing.
Josephine: Oh! Mummy, could we please?
Mrs Russell: I'm not really sure, they might be in the way.
Evgenia: Do not worry Mrs Russell, I will look after them, like a Susan. They will come to no harm.
Mrs Russell: Well, If you are sure?
Ransome: Then it is settled, we will start sailing lessons straight away. I'll soon make sailors of you.
EVERYONE STANDS UP AR, E AND MRS R MOVE OFF STAGE. THANK YOUS AND GOODBYES ALL ROUND. THEN SILENCE. G AND J STARE AT EACH OTHER FOR A FEW SECONDS THEN:
Josephine & George: Gosh!
CURTAIN

Scene 6 Postscript

Well, there it is. I've now shown you just a few of the people and circumstances that inspired one particular person to attain remarkable achievements from an inauspicious beginning.

Despite his worries and tribulations, including his long periods of ill-health, this young man won through, determined to achieve his dream even before he knew what that dream truly was.

[*ALL ENTER BEHIND*]

Arthur Michell Ransome is now famous; he is an Inspirational Enabler in his own right, and there are many, many people – you among them, I'm sure – who'll say 'Aye Aye' to that!

Goodbye!

[*STEP BACK. CURTAIN, TROIKA MUSIC, BOW SINGLY FROM R, ALL BOW, CURTAIN*]

THE SPARKINSON INTERVIEWS

Sparkinson interviews Missee Lee and the GA

After Brian's triumph in 2001, we looked to him for further insights. That was how we acquired the first of the Sparkinson Interview series. We believe his interviewees supplied some of their own background too. At that time, Michael Parkinson had been hosting a very long-running series of interviews on BBC television; our host at Southampton was Professor Brian Sparkes, so the play on words was obvious.

This was again first put on for the Southern Region, but Brian was persuaded to produce new versions, including one for the 2007 IAGM, when Southern Region's turn had come round again. So this is the version that follows:

RANSOME CENTRE STAGE

The Sparkinson interviews on BBC Radio conducted by Brian Sparkinson.

A play based on an interview with James Turner talking about his latest book 'Mixed Moss by a Rolling Stone' and we will also hear from other guests who had a part to play in the writing of this best-selling adventure book.

This play has been produced twice owing to the inclusion of an extra guest and a change in some actors taking part.

To avoid any confusion, a list of the players will be shown at the end of this introduction. Here is a list of the actual participants with a brief description of their connection with Mr. Turner.

As reported in the *Radio Times*, the Sparkinson interviews.

Interviewer	Brian Sparkinson, tall, slim, charming man, a favourite with the ladies.
James Turner	Adventurer, sailor, writer and traveller.
Molly Blackett	Long suffering Mother of two wild daughters and her Brother, James, lives in a big house near Windermere.
Lt. Col. Jolys DSO	Slightly rotund, retired soldier, good-hearted warrior. Useful man to have around.
Mrs. Walker	Mother of five, lost her parents when still young. Travelled to Australia where she met and married a young English naval officer and returned to England.
Miss Maria Turner	A great aunt, Victorian in her ways, lives in Harrogate. Good pianist. Has fixed ideas on the behaviour of children and grownups.

THE SPARKINSON INTERVIEWS

Missee Lee	Absolute ruler of Dragon Island which lies off the coast of China together with two other islands. Missee Lee very small, very young but very brave. Excellent sailor, educated in England. Loves Latin which is just as well.
"Too Low"	One time 'warm up' man. All time bodyguard. Too Low was given his name by his Mother because he was very small for a man-child. Even when full grown he was smaller than most men but had great speed and strength in the art of defence and attack and so became the devoted personal bodyguard to Missee Lee, the twenty-two gong Taicoon of Dragon Island.

When Miss Lee came to England to visit her *alma mater*, she also agreed to appear on the radio show called the Sparkinson Interviews.

As Too Low would not leave her side, he was given the 'warm up' job for the studio audience. Despite being a complete novice, he had a charm about him and with his broken English, captivated the audience.

Yes, Too Low had charm and smiled a lot, yet men would cross the road and bow in deference when seeing him coming.

His love of birds and animals and his happy smile concealed his other self – the most dangerous man of the three islands.

RANSOME CENTRE STAGE

<u>The Cast list.</u>
The persons who appeared in the original interview are played by actors as follows:
James Turner by Paul Crisp
Mrs Molly Blackett by Jill Goulder
Lt Col Jolys by Gilbert Satterthwaite
Mrs Mary Walker by Judith Powell
Missee Lee (1st showing) by Jill Goulder
Missee Lee (2nd showing) by Hilary Weston
Sparkinson by Brian Sparkes
Too Low by Brian Hopton

Finally, the Producers of this Sparkinson Interview offer their grateful thanks, and indeed that of the studio audience, to Tony Parslow, for the magnificent reproductions of the Three Island banners.

... and James Turner

THE SPARKINSON INTERVIEWS

This is Brian Sparkinson speaking. Thank you listeners for tuning in to my show and thank you too, to the studio audience who have come to watch the show going out live today.

I have an impressive guest list for you, consisting of Mrs Mary Walker, Mrs Mary Blackett, Lt Colonel Tom Jolys, Miss Maria Turner and our special guest, Miss Lee all the way from China. They all have quite an extraordinary connection with my first guest... if I were to mention exotic places such as Zanzibar, Rio de Janeiro or Casablanca to him, he would hardly raise an eyebrow. He has been in most of them around the world, and now he has written a best selling autobiography about his life spent 'knocking up and down' as he puts it.

He is here to tell us just a little about that and how his book almost never made it to the printers ... please welcome James Turner ..... Hello James .

Hello to you, I'm very pleased to be here and to see some of my friends and relatives.

Now James, a night in a police cell and leaving Oxford before they sent you down, not a very auspicious start.

No... well the night of internment was nothing really. Boat Race night you know. Oxford prevailed and the order of the day was a Bobbie's helmet at all costs, I got the helmet but unfortunately they got me. Fined five quid.

Academically I was a poor student, too Gung Ho, I preferred to learn on my feet, 'hands on' so to speak.

So what happened next?

Packed a bag, said my goodbyes and got a job on a steamer bound for New York and after what seemed like a hundred jobs, I landed one with International Oil as an office boy and worked my way up to personal assistant to one of the top executives. This enabled me to travel to some pretty outlandish places, drilling for oil, there were some hairy moments here and there, some of the local lads took exception to us being in their backyard. Anyhow after a few years of that I got itchy feet. I had heard a lot of talk among the old hands about gold in some of the places we had worked, so I thought, why not? Grab a few bags of the yellow stuff and I'd be made for life. Well let me tell you prospecting is not all it's made out to be, it's a hard, miserable and dangerous existence.

Did you find any gold?
About enough to pay my way, but gold's a funny thing, it drives you crazy. The big paydirt is always just ahead, only when you get to where you think it is, it's moved on again and if you do hit the bonanza there are a hundred men waiting to steal it from you, kill you if need be.

Where did most of this prospecting take place?
South America seemed a good place. The Incas had tons of the stuff you know. They even used it for drain pipes. Trouble is it's a hell of a place to travel in so I hired a sea-going boat, thirty six footer, a bit basic but good enough for the job. When I was with International Oil I met a young chap, Timothy Stedding, he had worked for a Mining Company and was very knowledgeable when it came to mining, very misleading young fellow, very quiet and shy until the chips were down and I might tell you they were down on more than one occasion. Anyhow, he was also fed up with his job and so I talked him into

coming on the big adventure with me. We rigged the boat out with everything we could think of and set sail for the Americas. We went down the Channel, through the Bay of Biscay, stopping only at the Canaries for fresh food and water and then straight through to Pernambuco. We then worked our way down the coast making forays up the small rivers when we came across them, panning for gold.
Did you find any?
Oh yes, but not much.
Were you troubled by natives?
Not much, you could see them flitting around some times, but we were armed and I found the best thing to do was to let a couple of shots off into the trees, that made them have second thoughts about trying anything. Except there was one time when we had to moor in a river. We normally anchored offshore but that night the sea was very rough and we were surrounded by sandbanks. It was a good thing I remembered something I had read in Joshua Slocum's great book 'Sailing Alone Around the World' when stocking up for the voyage, so I included a bag of carpet tacks in the stores. On going to bed we scattered them around the deck. Good thing natives don't wear shoes. About three in the morning there was a lot of howling and hopping up on deck, the blighters had come up silently and crept aboard.
What happened next?
I threw open the forward hatch and let them have both barrels of my old elephant gun, straight up into the night sky. The result was instantaneous, they all dived over the edge as one and made for the shore leaving us with three

very good dug-out canoes. We hauled one up on deck next morning as it might have come in useful.

The upshot of that was that we felt we had pushed our luck as far as it would go, we had a bit of gold to keep us going for a while so we headed back to Rio, stocked the boat and back to England.

But you were not ready to settle down?

Good Lord no, I went back to the Lakes for a while and stayed with Molly but it wasn't long before the old feet started to itch again and I tried my hand at Big Game Hunting.

Big game in Africa?

Yes, it was latest craze of the bored rich, they had nothing better to do than have their picture taken standing on a dead elephant, grinning their heads off. I wasn't very enamoured with it but I figured that if I wasn't doing it, someone else would. Besides I did my best to see that they killed as little as possible by turning up when the beasts had gone. They put it down to my incompetence.

Did you shoot anything yourself?

Only once, a lioness, it was her or me I'm afraid to say, I was the intended main course for dinner that night. It wasn't a great job but I met a lot of nice people over there and the sunsets over the Serengeti have to be seen to be believed.

I gave that a couple of years then I chucked it and started on archaeology.

Archaeology, that was rather a change of direction was it not?

Which ever way the wind blew I went with it, Carnarvon

had just discovered the tomb of Tutankhamen and the world went wild, everything went Egyptian, including me. I read every book I could find on the subject and joined in the digging, got well paid for it too, but my God it was hot, Karnak must be one of the hottest places on earth, not counting Alice Springs, but that's another story. Did I find any artifacts? No, not really, just one or two bits and pieces that now hang in my houseboat that I keep on the lake.

Ah! yes the houseboat, that's where you wrote your autobiography 'Mixed Moss *by a Rolling Stone.'*
That's right it was, it took me a whole year or more and I can honestly say it was the toughest job I have ever undertaken. Plus the fact that my two young nieces would not leave me alone for one moment, the trouble was that the summer before I had bought them a sailing dinghy which we named *Amazon* mainly because I said they were like the legendary young Amazons of South America, but much fiercer. In revenge for me ignoring them they tried to blow up my boat with a large firework and unfortunately I came to completely the wrong conclusion and blamed another set of children who were camping nearby. Shortly after that I had to go to London on business and while I was away some villains broke into the houseboat, smashed it up and took away my trunk that had been with me on most of my travels. My manuscript was in it together with all my diaries. Well that was it, I was ready to give the whole thing up and concentrate on having some fun. I had made up with my nieces and became friends with the Walker children and one day we all went whaling: fishing

actually, except Titty and Roger. Titty, bless her heart, was convinced my treasure as she called it was buried on a small island nearby, and blow me down it was, the burglars couldn't get it open and were coming back later. I left them a note, 'honesty is the best policy', let's hope they took notice.

So this is where we came in, your book was published and is already into a fourth edition in just a year and a half.

Yes I have been very lucky one way and another and I have said many times, never again, but you know these old feet of mine are beginning to itch once more, but I have had so much fun with those young ones that perhaps I just might put pen to paper again and write another book. In fact there are enough stories to fill several books and I hardly need leave the old houseboat. I have come to realise that home is where the heart is. So I think I might let my fingers do the travelling and give my poor feet a rest from now on. Now I'm sure you've had enough of my ramblings, you have all been very patient.

Not at all it has been fascinating... My thanks to James Turner for giving us here and all our listeners at home just a glimpse of what his book is all about and I'm sure that anyone reading it will look forward to his next book, which sounds as if it will be a subject much nearer to home......

Well there you have it, a brief insight into James Turner's amazing life, up to now at any rate, and if you want to know more then I suggest you buy his book, 'Mixed Moss by a Rolling Stone'. It really is a very good read.

Further to and following on from the book came another set of adventures that also involved my other guests in some way and another.....My second guest is one of those people who always seem to be in the background and yet are essential to any plan or expedition .... Please welcome the mother of the children who rescued the original 'Mixed Moss' manuscript which James described as the hardest thing he had ever done and had put the best of his life into it...Mrs Mary Walker.

Mrs Walker, welcome to the show –
Thank you very much I am very pleased to be here.
Now before I ask you about your involvement in these tales of adventure, tell us a little about yourself.
Well..Waltzing Matilda will have given you a good clue, although I was born in the South of England, Redhill

actually and when my parents were alive we spent a lot of time in the Lakes, staying at farms, that is why we were holidaying there when all this started...but when I was about fifteen tragedy struck, I lost both my parents to diphtheria in a matter of weeks, it was a terrible time and my aunt and uncle, Beth and Bob were my nearest living relatives and they lived in Sydney, Australia.

How terrible, what became of you after that?
I was taken into care for a while until my wonderful Aunt Beth came all the way from Australia by boat to take me to their home near Sydney Harbour and I spent three wonderful years there and discovered that I had a pack of distant cousins that I didn't know existed. We had a wonderful time together, they taught me to sail and I just loved it, we sailed in the Harbour. When I think of it I took an awful lot of risks, always thought I knew best. One day I capsized my cousin's boat entirely due to my stubborn insistence that I was right...I'm sure the wind that day was in a bad temper. Still, I think those experiences made me a better person, well I hope so anyway.

It says here that you spent time on a sheep farm
Yes! I spent every long summer holiday on one not far from Sydney. It is nothing like our Lakeland sheep farms, there were miles and miles of land and you needed a horse to get around it all. I just loved it but it could be dangerous, you could easily get lost, lucky for me my horse knew the way home, he took good care of me. The bush creatures were fascinating, kangaroos and opossums, the snakes could be very dangerous though.

Then you were eighteen and your life changed again.
Yes, the British Fleet entered Sydney Harbour for a Goodwill Tour and there were great celebrations, one of

which was a Grand Ball for all the British Officers. Uncle Bob worked at the shipyards and he wangled me a ticket. It was supposed to be only for the dignitaries and their families. It was a wonderful Ball and I had a new dress specially for the occasion.
And this is where you met your husband to be?
I had been asked to dance a couple of times and I was just standing watching the dancing when somebody said,
'I would very much like to have the next dance with you, may I?' I turned round and there was this tall, slim young man with a very tanned face and startling blue eyes, all crinkly in the corners, as he smiled at me. We had the next dance of course and the next and the next, in fact I did not leave his side for the rest of the evening. Yes...I think I can say that I was swept off my feet. Ten days later we were married by the ship's Padre, just two days before his ship sailed and two months later I was in Portsmouth, England to begin my married life.
Ted was only a Sub-lieutenant then and we lived in Naval quarters. That was twenty-five years ago, Ted's a Captain now and we have a large house in Falmouth, there are seven of us now when Ted's home on leave, not counting Polly the Parrot and Sinbad the Cat. There is also Gibber the Monkey but he's in a Zoo, thank goodness.
That is a really amazing story and I don't want to leave it, but can I come to the holiday that began the whole saga.
Yes, we had travelled up from the South by train to stay at Holly Howe where I had stayed as a child. As soon as the children saw the island they wanted to sail off and camp on it, John and Susan had done a lot of sailing, but Ted is

the Captain so I wrote to ask him what he thought. Typical Ted he sent this telegram.

`BETTER DROWNED THAN DUFFERS IF NOT DUFFERS WONT DROWN`

Basically it meant yes, so off they went and soon met up with two girls who also had a boat and started to have lots of adventures. One of which was capturing each others boat. My lot had *Swallow* and the two girls had *Amazon*. To cut the story short Titty, my third eldest, captured *Amazon* in the middle of the night and while she had the boat anchored, heard two men burying what she thought was treasure. Titty has a marvellous imagination, in reality it turned out to be James's trunk stolen from his Houseboat and, more importantly, the manuscript for his book.

And so began this friendship between your children, James and the two local children who turned out to be his nieces, the daughters of his sister Mrs Molly Blackett.

Yes and he has been very generous in return over the next few years. He paid to repair *Swallow* when she was damaged and took them all on a world cruise which almost ended in disaster, which I think you are going to hear about a little later. Next summer there are great plans to sail around the Western Isles of Scotland but I shall have to consult Ted about it.

Now you have never actually been involved in any of the adventures apart from supplying food and comfort to the adventurers.

No, I had to look after Bridget who was very young at the time and I have had to sit and suffer especially when they were with Jim Brading on the *Goblin* sailing on the Orwell, or so I thought, when in fact they were out to sea, although it was not really their fault. But if I had known what was really happening, well I dread to think of it. Then another time they were camping at Hamford Water in Suffolk and this time Bridget went with them. The idea was to survey and map the area but the Blackett girls turned up and they also teamed up with another group and the whole thing turned into an unholy war. In spite of all that they did manage to get the surveying done and all returned unharmed, thank goodness.

It would seem that although your children are well brought up and well behaved they appear to get into the most awful scrapes, why do you think this is?

I don't really know, it seems to just happen, things start out all perfectly as planned then things start to go wrong. It is almost as if someone is controlling events and making things happen, still the main thing is that all ends well. There were other holidays when neither Ted or I were there, when perfectly normal holidays turned into pretty unusual ones.

For instance?

Well it was Winter time and poor Ted had been away since Bridget was born so I just had to go to Malta where he was stationed so that he could get a peep at her. So what better time to send the rest of them up to Holly Howe for the Winter holidays. Little did I know that it would turn into a Polar expedition with all the dangers that can entail. The lake froze over and some of their friends got lost in a blizzard and my lot went out after them. Everybody ended up at what they called the North Pole and there was Ted, Bridget and me in sunny Malta completely oblivious to what was going on. Then there was the gold mining.

Gold mining?

RANSOME CENTRE STAGE

Evidently James here and his friend Timothy Stedding were in South America prospecting for gold or something. I was at home with Bridget who had a very bad case of whooping cough so my lot had to stay with Mrs Blackett until I could join them, owing to the fact that the Jacksons at Holly Howe already had visitors. The Blackett girls had this great idea that they could find gold much nearer to home. In fact on High Topps above Beckfoot, their family home. They knew this old chap Slater Bob who spun them a yarn about gold in the hills, so off they went all eight of them, the Callum children were also with them. Did I not mention them? Dick and Dorothea, Dick is very scientific, Dorothea very dreamy but very nice children. Anyway! they had a tremendous time. There was a severe drought and they had no water on High Topps but they divined for it, Titty was the only one who could do it. She seems to have these gifts and found the water just where they wanted to camp. They spent a long time prospecting for this gold without success and then, quite by accident Roger found it, or rather what they all thought was gold. He was messing about as Roger does and he tumbled into a small ravine and found an old working. He spotted a crack in the rock, banged at it and a large piece fell off and there was the gold, only it was copper.
Copper?
Yes, they crushed some, panned it and smelted it hoping to have a small ingot to show James on his return and that is when everything went horribly wrong.
I have to confess that I know nothing about mining and smelting. Tell us what went wrong.

THE SPARKINSON INTERVIEWS

Well as I said it was copper, not gold and after hours of smelting the sample disappeared.
Evidently gold can only be dissolved in something called, 'AQUA REGIA'. Dick knew this and went off to Beckfoot to experiment in James's study. At this point James arrived home from South America to find Dick in his study saying they had found gold and it must be gold because it had dissolved in Aqua Regia. The problem was that almost anything will dissolve in this stuff, proving nothing. Anyway James had a look at the samples and pronounced it to be copper, which is what he really wanted. 'Gold drives men crazy and is best left alone', he said. Then a most serious thing happened, Fell fire.
Fire! Was it all that smelting, did the children start it?
No, no but they initially got the blame and were fighting it when James arrived with Dick swiftly followed by Colonel Jolys and his band of firefighters and after a long battle it was out. The only casualty was Roger who burnt his hand slightly. Mind you there was a lot that went on that I know nothing about, which is just a well. Grown-ups are known as natives to these children of mine and evidently we are not to be trusted, so that is about as much as I can tell you, but I'm sure your other guests have tales to tell and I don't want to give too much away.
Well I could go on listening for hours but unfortunately we do not have the time. My thanks to Mrs Mary Walker for telling me and all our listeners about her early life and the exploits of her imaginative and adventurous children, and may things continue to go well for you all. Thank you.

My third guest on the programme is one of those of us who

serves their country unsung, whether it be in this country or one of the most dangerous places in this world. Please welcome the now retired but still very active, Lt. Colonel Tom Jolys DSO.

Now, Colonel Jolys, welcome to my programme. I trust you had a good journey down from the lakes?
Yes thank you, trains were on time as of course they should be.
Now you were a career soldier serving mostly in the Middle-East, tell us something about that.
Well I was educated at Rugby you know, I did fairly well but never fancied a job behind a desk somewhere in a stuffy office. We men in the family had always been in the services going way back. My father made Major General

and served with distinction in the first Afghan war of 1878. Whereas my grandfather was a navy man, who was killed in action during the taking of the Taku Forts off the China coast in 1842. So it was only natural that I followed the family tradition. On leaving school I became an officer cadet at Sandhurst and served my time there with distinction. I then left England as a Bengal Lancer to serve with the Indian Army. . .Actually I had hoped to go to Kneller Hall and become a military trumpeter, but I failed the audition. I think I was pretty good, but Father didn't approve and I've always suspected he put the kybosh on it.
You never married I believe.
No, no there were girls of course, especially when I was younger but I thought it not really fair on a wife of a soldier on almost permanent active service, the army was my wife and family. As for now, well I suppose I am too much set in my ways, bit of an old grouch you might say.
Now I know you are very modest when it comes to your exploits but we would like to know something about them.
As I said I went to serve in the Indian Army and I was involved in the North West Frontier Campaign, fighting against the Pathans, damn fierce lot they were, best not to get captured by them. We were still horse soldiers then as the name suggests, still charging in like the old Light Brigade. There was a lot of skirmishing around the Khyber Pass area, that was where I won my DSO in 1908. It was later presented to me by the then Viceroy of India, Lord Minto. Mind you there were a lot of lads who deserved it as much or more than I did. Things don't always work out the way they should in the British Army it's the class

system at work you know. There were other momentous occasions at which I was present. The Regiment was represented at the funeral procession of Queen Victoria in 1901, I felt very honoured to be taking part in that homage to a great Queen, then in 1911 we formed part of the March Past at the succession of King George V as Emperor of India at the Delhi Durbah, that was a great day, full dress uniform you know.

But you were not confined to India during your service days?
No we were very much involved in the Palestine business and guarding the Suez Canal.
Then there was Mesopotamia and Gallipoli against the Turks, that was a bloody war. We fought a lot of that as dismounted troops because of the terrain, horses were on the way out anyway, things were changing fast, it was the beginning of the end of an era.
We finally overcame the Turks after Jerusalem and in September 1918 we marched triumphantly into Damascus.
During all that time I never received so much as a scratch, but the mosquitos got me in the end I'm afraid, you could hide from the bullets but not from those little devils. The malaria got to me and they pensioned me off at the age of forty-five.
I went back to the lakes and bought a little cottage which a woman cleans once a week for me, otherwise I look after myself.

You retired from the army but not from active life.
That's right, soon got fed up just hanging around,

gardening and so on. It wasn't long before I became a Justice of the Peace and a local councillor, that takes up quite a bit of my time. Then I was invited to become Master of the Hunt for the area, but there was still something missing, then one day during a long hot spell there was a fell fire, fortunately it wasn't too serious but nothing was done, there is no fire service within miles. So I thought, why not start a volunteer fire and emergency service. People are very much on their own up there you know, hardly anyone has a telephone, it could be hours before help would arrive so I organised a group of the younger lads to listen for the coach horn signal, when they heard the signal they in turn would sound their horns and rendezvous at my cottage in cars or lorries. It has been quite successful, saving one or two valuable properties. Of course the men make a bit of fun of me and my military ways behind my back, they think I don't know they privately call me Sergeant Major Jolys, but I don't mind. I have been called a lot worse in the army by the lower orders. The main thing is that we get the job done and I think they take a bit of pride in doing it.
You had a bit of fire fighting to do with James here.
Yes, hadn't rained for weeks, fells were like tinder, some fool Trippers stopped for a picnic on the Dundale road, probably left a cigarette burning, came to admire the country and promptly destroyed it. If it hadn't been for those children sending a pigeon to Beckfoot so that James here could warn me we would have been too late, the farm buildings would have gone as well. Those children were very resourceful, pigeons eh! I remember we used to use

them in the military, brings back a few memories that does.

Then there was an occasion when you and your men went on a bit of a goose chase looking for a missing person.

Hrrump, yes I remember that rather too well as will some of the other leading lights of the districts namely the Postman, the Doctor and most of the local police force. I was dozing in my deckchair when a call came through from Beckfoot, it was Miss Ruth going on about her Great Aunt Maria who had gone off in James's car with Billy Lewthwaite driving. Billy was so frightened of her that he forgot to check for fuel, consequently they soon ran out of the stuff, She sent him back with a flea in his ear to get some. However when he got back she was gone. He looked around for her, found nothing so drove back to the house.

THE SPARKINSON INTERVIEWS

As I said Miss Ruth came on the telephone to report her missing. I swung into action, called up my men in the usual manner and spread them around they lake, I told them to use the old hunting call if they spotted anything...View Halloooo.
And did you find her?
I had my men all round the lake and by this time the police were also involved, Billy's brother Sammy being the local Bobby called in his Sergeant and another Constable to join the search. Then some of my men spotted her in a small sailing boat with two children, heading for Beckfoot, so everyone went back there and gathered on the lawn, including the Postman and the Doctor who were worried about something. Up they came to the lawn and I helped the lady out.
Was she pleased and grateful for everyone's concern?
Pleased! Grateful! I should say not, she started on me first, I've been under fire many a time but this was a barrage like I had never before experienced, by the way she's not here today is she?....Then she laid into the other protagonists one by one, she was that mad, but I took most of the blame. The main thing was that she was safe. Not long after that she left to catch her train, I offered to take her in my car but she would not have it, but although heavily defeated I went down all guns blazing, so to speak and sent her off with three rousing cheers and a mighty blast from all the hunting horns.
And after all that?
Well I continue to sit on the Bench, do my Council work, hunt with the hounds and doze in my deckchair, half

RANSOME CENTRE STAGE

hoping the telephone will ring but on the other hand hoping it will not, because it usually means that some poor soul is in trouble.

Well, time is pressing and I must move on with my thanks to Lt Colonel Tom Jolys who is living proof that soldiers do not simply fade away but continue to serve their country even in times of peace.........

Ladies and Gentlemen

My next guest is someone who has been much maligned as an interfering matriarchal busybody, but according to her she was only doing her bounden duty and in doing so she created adventures for the Walker, Callum and Blackett children.

So here to tell her side of the story is the Blacketts' great aunt, Miss Maria Turner.

THE SPARKINSON INTERVIEWS

Miss Turner welcome to the show. I trust you had an uneventful journey from the north?
No I most certainly did not, the train was crowded and my compartment was filthy, I had reserved a First Class seat at enormous cost and ended up having to tidy it myself. It reminded me of the disgraceful state that I found my nephew's houseboat in, when I was trying to find out what was going on behind my back during those school holidays.
Yes, now according to my notes Mrs Blackett had gone on holiday with her brother to recover from influenza, leaving her daughters Ruth and Margaret alone apart from their cook.
That is correct, or as I thought at the time, I now know that there were two other children at the house and everything that happened now makes perfect sense.
But the cook was in charge, was there any real reason for you to drop everything and travel to the lakes?
There most certainly was, my nieces, Ruth in particular, were becoming most unlike the ladies they should have been growing up to be. I had noticed that Ruth was getting very bossy and domineering. I do not know where she gets it from, probably from that itinerant nephew of mine. He has always been a bit of a black sheep you know.
So you arrived and everything seemed quite normal?
At first, the girls were very well behaved, although that, in hindsight, should have aroused my suspicions and then odd things started to happen.
What things?
First there was the apple pie, we had just a small amount

and I requested that the cook keep it for the next day only to find she had cut it up and covered it with custard and served it as if in a working class cafeteria. A more surly and uncooperative woman you would find it hard to meet...and then there was this man, a tramp I thought, every time we came face to face he would dive over a wall or something just as ridiculous. Then there was the postman, I watched him creep up the path to the door, ram the letters through the letterbox and then take to his heels. The doctor was no better he treated me as if I was an unexploded bomb.

Then I believe you confronted a burglar?
Yes, or so I thought...we had all gone to bed and the girls were asleep, as far as I knew. Then I heard small noises from down stairs so I went to investigate only to find that the window of James's study had been left open, probably by that irresponsible cook. I then returned to my bed only to hear the study window shoot up making a horrible noise. I looked out of the window to see this figure scurrying away in the moonlight. Of course I now know that it was only the boy hiding away from me in the woods with his sister.

Evidently he had been hiding in the boot box which for some reason had the word Timothy written across it and when I shut the window he had to open it again. It appears that he was after some equipment for my tramp who was in fact a friend of my nephew who had permission to use the houseboat and equipment anyway, but for some reason he was frightened to come to the house..I cannot see why but then everyone seemed to be behaving in a very

peculiar fashion.
What if, at the time, you had found out what was going on?
Well the parents of the children were away on business so I would not have sent them away. They would have stayed at the house and been looked after in a civilised way instead of living like cavemen up in the woods.
Now I believe you had your suspicions about all this and went off on your own without telling anyone and were reported missing. Colonel Jolys here has already told us something about it.
I was never lost, it started with that idiot Lewthwaite not checking the vehicle for petrol. Fortunately a butcher's van came along while I was waiting for Lewthwaite to come back with the petrol and he took me almost to Swainson's farm where I suspected the Walker children and my nieces might be, I did not know then that it was two different children that were involved. They were not there and Mary Swainson kindly took me to the houseboat where I waited. I was horrified by the mess, the cabin was full of dirt and rocks, so I set to to give it a thorough clean. To cut a long story short I was given a lift back to Beckfoot by two children who turned out to be the very children I was looking for. They sailed their boat very well right up to the Beckfoot lawn, which was full of people shouting, cheering and sounding off horns. I could see straight away that Tommy Jolys was the instigator of all this foolery, marching about as if in charge of an army.
I believe you put quite a few people in their places?
They were all there on the lawn the police, the postman, the doctor, Tommy and his men all acting as if they were

back at school. Leaping around, blowing on horns and cheering. I suppose that they might have been glad that I was alive. I will give them the benefit of the doubt. But made sure that they were all firmly in their places, especially Tommy. He may look like a grown up but believe me inside he is still a little boy playing at soldiers. The cook had not made my sandwiches and I had little time to meet my train and to cap it all as I went into the house I spotted Mrs Lewthwaite's other son Samuel with my cloak. He had been allowing their bloodhounds to smell it. Well really I was all for writing to Mrs Lewthwaite to complain about her sons but thought better of it. They are good sons at heart, if a little slow and there was no real point in upsetting her.

Can I come to holiday tasks, knitting, reading aloud, reciting poetry and playing the piano. Is this really what children should do during their holiday?

When I was a small child we had to do all these things, also sit properly, speak properly, eat properly even walk properly. They did me no harm and I believe that I am better for it.

I think you must remember that anything I did, was for the best and I feel it is my duty to help my sister's daughter in every way I can, especially after the loss of Robert, her dear husband when she was left to bring them up on her own. James here has a good heart, but he's an adventurer and a wanderer. Liable to forget the niceties of life. Girls need to be ladies not tomboys.

Yes, but having said that, and according to my notes, you were a very sporty type at school – it says here that you

were a Wimbledon junior at tennis.
That is so, but that was a very long time ago.
It was also thought that you might have become a professional piano player, but you opted for a career in teaching, specializing in Latin, it says here.
Ah! well, *que sera sera*, whatever will be will be.
So, thank you for giving your side of a very interesting tale but before we finish, I believe that one of the holiday tasks Ruth had to perform was to play Chaminade on the piano?
That is entirely correct, although it did not come easy to her.
Well we have a piano here and I just happen to have a piece of Chaminade sheet music. Would you play it for us?
Well I may be a little out of practice but I will try. I would never ask the girls to do something I could not do myself.

RANSOME CENTRE STAGE

My last guest is somebody who is a strange composition of the highest classical education mixed and fermented with an occupation that in Britain last flourished more than three hundred years ago .. piracy – or, as I am bound to be corrected, protection of shipping... From somewhere off the coast of China, Ladies and Gentlemen, please welcome the undisputed queen of her profession... Miss Lee.

Miss Lee, welcome to England. I believe that this is not your first visit?
No, I come here as young girl to school – Great Marlow – and to study at Cambridge – Classical Latin. Now I am back to visit old university, and perhaps see Boat Race; of course Cambridge will win – Oxford very poor rowing, very poor degree... very good marmalade.

THE SPARKINSON INTERVIEWS

May we talk about your part in the extraordinary saga when the boat called the Wildcat *caught fire, and James here and the children had to take to the lifeboats? Consequently James and the Blackett girls were picked up by a junk belonging to one of your taicoons, Chang, while the Walkers landed but were also captured by Chang's men.*

Yes, indeed. First I hear of it, my amah tell me sleepers at temple on island, and I saw my Latin book with English writing. Then I hear that more people with Chang, and he plan to ransom. So I signal to Chang 'Bring all these people'. I want to meet these English who know Latin.

And what happened when you met them?

First I see this gentleman, Mr. Turner. Big disappointment – no Latin, not even Cambridge. Then I see the children. I ask them 'Do you know where you are on map?' Prisoners who know where we are on map go back, tell where Three Islands are, gunboats come; so, if they know, [makes chop-head sign].

You wouldn't have chopped the children's heads off, would you surely, Miss Lee?

My father made rule in Three Islands: no English prisoners, because English make trouble with gunboats. But – these children might be fulfilment of my dream. Latin – ah, Latin. I love it so – Virgil, Ovid – and I want to teach it.

Why didn't you stay in England and teach Latin there?

I love my days at Cambridge, and had great sorrow when I was called back by my father. He great man, head of all islands; he knew he was dying, and wanted me to take his place. Great responsibility for me, keeping Three Islands

from fighting between themselves; so no more Cambridge. Then, when I see these children, I see whole class of students, to teach forever, Classical Latin.
So you intended to keep them for ever and teach them... Latin?
Yes. I negotiate with Chang. He is small taicoon – 10-gong only. I am head of Three Islands – 22-gong taicoon - and I say to him 'I keep children here forever – so no gunboats'.
And James here?
Chang kept Mr. Turner because he is very rich – Lord Mayor of San Francisco – he will ask for ransom. Later, Chang discover not rich, wants to chop head; and the children – my Latin class – say they cannot work if Mr. Turner in prison; so – I buy him, from Chang.
So you started to teach your class. What happened next?
Ah, I had some moments of disappointment – big moments. Still, Roger very good student, rest not very good, but plenty of time to improve. Mr. Turner – Oxford education – no good at Latin. Omnium stultissimi sunt senes.
Sed tu, magistra, nullo modo stulta.
Ita vero. [To Capt. Flint]. You agree, of course, Mr. Turner? [Flint blushes and mumbles.]
So you must have had a difficult time with your students – except Roger.
In fact, no! After a few days, suddenly they become model students. Learned hard, very good, all of them. I think to myself – so, why have they changed? – but I know they cannot get away and I am happy.
I gather that you gave your model students a treat.

THE SPARKINSON INTERVIEWS

Ah yes, the little dragon. Three Islands dragon festival happening quite soon, and I decide to give my good students their own dragon for festival; reward for hard work. Also I gave them holiday expedition, in my junk *Shining Moon*, to the island of my father's temple.
That must have been a nice break for you all.
Yes, but bad outcome. On way home from island, I visit Taicoon Wu with my students. Wu is old seaman, and sees that Mr. Turner carries a sextant, collected from the children's possessions on the island. Wu knew that with sextant Mr. Turner could locate Three Islands for gunboats...
What happened next?
Things very bad. Chang and Wu very unhappy. Chang sent back the money that I paid for Mr. Turner: so he is now Chang's prisoner not mine; Chang free to kill him, Chang and Wu want to kill all my students. So I think hard, very hard. What to do?
I think it was a difficult decision for you, Miss Lee.
Yes, yes, so hard. But I cannot let my model students be killed – even Mr. Turner here – and I cannot let Three Islands fight again. I think of my father. My way is clear. No more Cambridge, no more Latin classes. I am Missee Lee, 22-gong taicoon of Three Islands.
And – I know because the children are all here safely, as is James – you found a way for them to escape.
I trusted my students not to reveal to British Navy where Three Islands are. I thought – how to let them escape from Chang and Wu's men who are watching? Then I remembered: dragon feast soon, and children had been repairing

old dragon, to take part in parade. What better than to slip out in dragon costume? Everybody having good time, no-one notice little dragon dancing through streets, down to water late at night.

And then you needed to get them off the island and away.

Yes; so I sacrifice my beautiful little junk *Shining Moon*, for my students – my friends. They can reach England in her no problem.

You were a very good friend to them, Miss Lee. sacrificing Shining Moon!

You know, I liked to think of my *Shining Moon* making journey to England. But – England – Cambridge – oh – very, very hard to turn back on my Cambridge dream. I have to remind myself that I am Chinese lady 'pirate', as Nansee says. Famous throughout Eastern seas. Everybody afraid. With good reason.

So, the model students joined the dragon festival, and slipped down to Shining Moon *and set sail. But that wasn't the end of the story, I think?*

No, indeed. They were missed quite soon, and Chang and Wu put the log boom across the river to stop them. So they thought of the gorge.

The gorge? Was that a way out?

But very difficult – full of rocks and swift currents – even in daytime, and now it is dark, dark. But they try; very brave – Mr. Turner show what he is worth – but I know they cannot. So I take the tiller.

You were on board? But surely – ?

Yes, in moment of weakness I forget my responsibilities. I want to be in Cambridge once again, so I hid in cabin, to go with them. But then the gorge time comes, so I show myself, and take *Shining Moon* through. Then, when in open sea, we are becalmed. Chasing junks get near enough to fire cannons, so I raise my dragon flag and they stop. Then I see there is fighting in Dragon Town; Chang

and Wu are fighting to see who will be twenty-two gong Taicoon. My path of duty now became clear. No more Cambridge. I say goodbye to my students and go back to take my rightful place as head of Three Islands.
And that you did, and you are now back here for a short holiday.
Yes, and I have been very happy to meet all my students again. All growing up, all doing very well – though Mr. Turner here growing out not up; but I am very happy to

meet him again too. Good sailor, bad university.
Well, I have to say that you have told us a truly amazing story. You know, it would make a very good book. Perhaps James here could write one as a follow-up to his autobiography?
I would like to thank all my guests for coming on to the show and giving us a thoroughly interesting account of the quite extraordinary events that have touched their lives. I would also like to thank the studio audience and all our listeners for joining us. So, until next time, it's goodbye from James Turner, Mrs. Mary Walker, Lt. Colonel Jolys, Maria Turner and the quite amazing Miss Lee, and of course myself... good evening to you all.

THE GREAT AUNT RETURNS AND LEAVES

This was first produced at a Southern Region meeting at Witley in 1995. When the Region was called on to produce an entertainment at the 2019 IAGM at Lyndhurst, it was decided to revive it. Brian tells us the background again, starting with the Witley performance:

I had never done anything like that before but it went so well. It was like watching real life.

The actors came on, spoke lines and left. The curtains opened and closed. *Scarab* came alongside and the doctor helped a very annoyed Great Aunt on to the stage where she flattened the nervous actors like skittles. Strike One! Strike Two! Who's next!

Then it was over with three million cheers. Then I was dragged on by the police. Was it that bad? No. People were clapping; happiness all round. Then it was over or was it?

Tony came up the gangplank and the bosun whistled him aboard.

So began twenty years of entertainment, local and national. Many years and lots of fun later, we came to Lyndhurst. A year and a half before that, I found myself saying "Let's do the *GA* again" but after all that time, I had problems. Tony was very ill and we had to have a new cast. Diana and Brian said they were too old and I respected that. Diana said she would like to do 'Eugenia' again but how could I incorporate it? Jill could not be Nancy now and she turned down the 'GA' but would love to be the cook. Judith Powell agreed to do the 'GA' but said it would be different. Andrew Silk had agreed to be Jolys but I pleaded with him to be 'Squashy Hat' instead. Although he was reluctant, he turned out to be the surprise of the day. Paul, despite having to run the entire weekend, agreed to do 'Jolys' again. Hilary took the lead as 'Nancy'. Very experienced in showbiz, as ever she was very good and held the play together. The

RANSOME CENTRE STAGE

Callums were played by my grandchildren, Daniel and Ella, and they did a good job. Peter Willis reprised his part as the sergeant and Alan Hakim made his debut as the doctor. Wendy Willis called the words of 'Peggy' off stage.

After eighteen months of trying, I could not fill the other three parts so I had to play them and one was a young boy. As I write this I am about to have my eighty fourth birthday! Still it was an attempt at a farce by Ransome. Everything considered, tiny stage, one rehearsal an hour before the start during which everything had to be set up. Jill Goulder had written a beginning and end to the play about what she, as Mrs. Blackett, found on her return from holiday which enriched the play no end.

Now how did I work in Diana Sparkes and her 'Eugenia' speech? Well I could not, but I recalled Ransome writing about Nancy taking over as he wrote S&A. From that I had the idea for a mini play. Ransome at his desk, Nancy appearing as his imaginary muse miming to the music of *Scheherazade* and putting ideas into his mind, as pictures from his story came up on the screen above his head. This was followed by 'Eugenia's' speech by Diana Sparkes which is about Ransome writing this story and her worries for the future.

The introduction is by David Middleton and the part of Ransome played by Brian Sparkes. The part of Nancy is acted and choreography by Hilary Weston to great effect. This mini play is derived from scene 4 of the play *Inspirations*, 'Slippers'.

I would like to take this opportunity to thank all the people who took part in these plays and all the people who helped to make them happen and to remember those who are no longer with us.

THE GA RETURNS AND LEAVES

Diana with the men who made her a star

A GIFT OF SLIPPERS

Lead in: read from stage, followed by Mime sequence, featuring Arthur Ransome at his desk. Pictures from S&A flash up on screen. Music and entry of imaginary Muse who helps him as he writes the story.......Mime ends.

Evgenia enters carrying water...sits at table on front of stage

Evgenia gives her thoughts on the situation.

CURTAINS CLOSE THE LEAD IN..... RANSOME AT HIS DESK...WRITING

RANSOME CENTRE STAGE

Narrator: Arthur Michell Ransome is at a crossroads. Earlier in his life, which has been, at times exciting and dangerous, he has earned his living as a journalist and writer of articles for books and newspapers.

He has acquired a new wife during his travels and now has to make a decision, which is not his alone to make.

Either he carries on as he is, eking out a living as a self-employed Freelancer, or he takes a nine-till-five job offered by his friend Ted Scott at the Guardian offices; which means forsaking his love of fishing and sailing, 'trapped in a corridor' as he describes it, and under pressure from his wife to have a more comfortable and steady life. He is putting off this decision as he tries to complete some articles on fishing.

THE GA RETURNS AND LEAVES

Strange how an ordinary occurrence, like a half-forgotten birthday, coincides with a gift of a pair of red slippers arriving at the wrong moment; can change everything. Suddenly he is distracted by laughter and the sight of his friend's four children running toward him waving the aforementioned slippers.

Later, after being rather curt with them, then becoming overcome with guilt, he decides to write them a short adventure story about four children in the Lakes.

So a story is born that will last for a hundred years. Here he is writing that story with the help of an imaginary Muse; who is it?

Evgenia, his Russian wife is impatient for the fishing articles to be ready, as they will earn money. The children's story can wait!

What followed was essentially the same as scene 4 of Inspirations *(p.37 above)*

and it was followed by the second performance of The GA Returns and Leaves:

RANSOME CENTRE STAGE

CAST 1998

Great Aunt	Diana Sparkes
"Cooky" – Mrs Braithwaite	Gill Gordon
Timothy Stedding	Aidan Musson
Nancy Blackett	Jill Goulder
The Sergeant	Peter Willis
Billy/Sammy Lewthwaite	Gilbert Satterthwaite
Jacky Warriner	Sam Waldrop
The Doctor	David Towne
Peggy Blackett	Eleanor Willis
Dorothea Callum	Paula Willis
Dick Callum	Katie Handasyde Dick
Colonel Jolys	Paul Crisp

CAST 2019

Molly Blackett	Jill Goulder
Great Aunt	Judith Powell
Cookie	Jill Goulder
Tim "Squashy Hat" Stedding	Andrew Silk
Nancy Blackett	Hilary Weston
The Sergeant	Peter Willis
Billy Lewthwaite }	
Jacky Warriner }	Brian Hopton
Sammy Lewthwaite }	
Doctor	Alan Hakim
Peggy Blackett	Wendy Willis
Dorothea Callum	Ella Hopton
Dick Callum	Daniel Hopton
Colonel Jolys	Paul Crisp

THE GA RETURNS AND LEAVES

Mrs Blackett: Hello everyone - I'd like to welcome you all very much to Beckfoot. My name's Molly Blackett, and I know that you're all already friends of my two outrageous girls, Ruth **[harrumph from offstage?]** (OOPS, Nancy) and Peggy. They've asked me (well, instructed, actually) to tell you a little about the entertainment that they've put on today. They said 'Well, we were all in the thick of it, but <u>you</u> got home after all of it and had to catch up, so you'll have a much better overall picture of it from everyone.' Well, heavens, I'm still reeling from all the tales! One thing that I will say is that I'd confidently expected that everything would go peacefully and that the girls and the Ds would cope absolutely splendidly at Beckfoot, on their own with Cook; and while the **<u>first</u>** part – about peacefully – didn't last for a moment, the second part truly did. I am so proud of them all. **[Cheers offstage].**

Well, a bit of background. I was really pretty ill for a while – summer 'flu is dreadful and knocks you back – and Jim (my brother, who is – well, Jim – but who's always been my rock and stay when it comes to it) just marched in with a plan of a sea voyage and a tour of the Scandinavian coast! But it meant being away for the first ten days of the girls' school holidays. But Jim persisted, and I saw his point, and the girls are a good independent pair, and Cook is a total **treasure** ... Well, so I went to see the girls at school and talked to them, and they so brightened at the thought of some **real** responsibility. Peggy's often crushed by Nancy, rather, but she just **blossomed** at being considered grown-up enough to run the house for a week or so. And it all worked so well about Dick and Dorothea; they were longing to get to the Lakes as soon as school ended, especially with their new sailing-boat just about ready; but their father was stuck in London for two weeks after that and the Dixons didn't have rooms free. When I heard, I wrote **straight** away to suggest that they came to Beckfoot for the first two weeks; that was what I'd have done anyway, but I thought that my girls would gain so much by being hosts to their friends rather than just rattling around on their own. Dick and Dorothea are both in their different ways such sensible children – I suppose that with their growing-up they've had to be quite grown-up – and I felt that being responsible for them would have a really good influence on my lovely wild girls. And Jim's colleague in the copper-mining enterprise, Timothy (who the girls disgracefully call Squashy Hat), was going to be here, working on sample analysis in a sort of laboratory that he and Jim have set up on Jim's houseboat, and he'd faithfully promised to look in regularly at Beckfoot. Then I'd be back, and Jim, and the Walkers were coming up just days after that, so it was all going to work out perfectly.

So off I went, and I was so happy thinking of everything working out; and I have to say that I really got back into proper health, just enjoying the sea air and the wonderful scenery. WELL! I got back, and Jim saw me installed at home and the girls were full of joy and there were Dick and Dorothea, and Cook ... But there was an extraordinary feel of electricity in the air, and of course I opened Aunt Maria's letter ...

Well, there was a **great** deal of explanation, and also a stream of visitors with astonishing tales – Col. Jolys, Sammy and Billy Lewthwaite, the doctor, the postman, the Swainsons –

THE GA RETURNS AND LEAVES

and Jim tearing back from seeing Timothy at the houseboat. Nancy showed me the first letter from Aunt Maria – goodness me – and told me about the telegrams, and one of the **worst** things was hearing how Cook had nearly left because of Aunt Maria's – well, approach. I found it hard to take in how very different things had been at Beckfoot from how I'd imagined. I did know, from an earlier visit by Aunt Maria that you probably know about, how she simply didn't understand how my girls were growing up to be strong independent young women in the modern age. She has her standards, and she certainly tried to impose them on me and Jim when we were young, but we keep them up in a different way now. Anyway, I learnt amidst all this that Dick and Dorothea had been installed in the old stone hut in the woods, learning a lot of new skills I gather (and so we all go up there for picnics now), and that Timothy had become a Suspicious Character to Aunt Maria because he'd done his typical thing of leaping over a wall to get away from people. There are a few elements that I haven't quite yet got to the bottom of – a burglary of some sort? – but I expect I'll hear about them eventually.

But it apparently all blew up when, just the day before Aunt Maria was to leave, she let my girls off the leash for the day as they'd been so good (darling girls – they did brilliantly), and they used their free day to go off happily with the Callum children and Timothy to the copper-mine to get some new samples for analysis. Now it seems that Aunt Maria had in her mind that Nancy and Peggy had been influenced for the bad by some particular children who'd been camping near here on her last visit. I'd tried to talk to her about it – to be honest, I slightly worried about the influence that my darling wild girls had had on beautifully-behaved Walker children! – but she was very fixed in this. And it turned out that on that day she'd decided to find out whether these bad children were in the area, and so she'd set off on some sort of search-and-destroy expedition while the girls were safely out of the way. What seems to have happened is that she ended up being taken to Jim's houseboat by Mary Swainson, as she thought that they must be there – but of course they weren't, as they weren't coming for another few days. So for everyone on land (Mary'd then gone off on holiday), she'd disappeared.

So I'll leave you here, with the play thought up originally by Dorothea but filled in by everyone else; as it opens, they're all happily out for the day, going to the mine; and then they get back and everything isn't right at all ...

SCENE 1
A FELLSIDE ABOVE BECKFOOT
The music JOHN PEEL is playing.
ENTER FROM RIGHT: NANCY, PEGGY, DICK, DOROTHEA & TIMOTHY, HOT FROM CLIMBING.
Throw off rucksacks and stop to take breath.
Nancy: *(looking back the way they've come).* It's almost too good to be true
Peggy: What is?
Nancy: <u>This</u>, of course. Don't you realise it's still morning? And we're not doing "holiday tasks". We're not mowing the lawn, we're not weeding, we're not winding wool, we're not thumping the beastly piano .... We can shiver our timbers without the Great Aunt's disapproval - and we haven't got to be back till suppertime. <u>It's as good</u>

<u>as if she didn't exist at all!</u>
Dot: Let's pretend <u>she's</u> a Pict, for a change
Nancy: And tomorrow she goes – and if she isn't pleased with us she ought to be. Nine days. Ten, counting tomorrow. And there hasn't been a single row (except for Cook giving notice). We've managed to do all the really important things in spite of her being here.
Dot: It'll feel funny when she's gone, not being Picts any more . . .
Tim: and not being a suspicious character – I don't like feeling shy of policemen.
Nancy: And not being angels – it's been jolly hard work being angels for nine whole days on end.
Tim: *(with an odd look at Nancy)* Let's look at your shoulders. You've had Dick and Dorothea in hiding all this time, you've roped in the postman and the milkman, and Cook and me and the Police and the Doctor, and tied us all up in knots and . . . let's see those shoulders
Nancy: *(moving away)* What's the matter with them?
Tim: *(chuckling to himself)* I can't see any wings on them, anyhow - but I wouldn't be surprised to find you had hoofs and a tail.
ALL THIS TIME, DOROTHEA HAS BEEN RATHER 'DISTANT'. NANCY NOTICES AND PUTS AN ARM ROUND HER.
Nancy: *(quickly changing the subject)* What is it Dot?
Dot: I was just wondering what was happening at Beckfoot
Nancy: She's solemnly packing. 'Cook, my black dress, please. Cook, that's not the way to fold it …. Now my shoes. No, no! Heel to toe. No, Cook, I think it will be

better if the dresses lie flat on top. And, Cook, I shall need those shoes this evening.' And poor old Cook's holding in until she's fit to bust. I told her she's simply got to hold in for just one more day.
Tim: Mmmm – I expect that's where the wings are!
Nancy: *(somewhat mortified)* I don't care what you say! We've never been so good for so long at a time in all our lives.
Dot: Let's try to forget her, just for a bit.
Nancy: Good.idea .... Forgotten. Wiped out. Done with. Gone .... Shiver my timbers. Let's get on. The S.A. & D. Mining Expedition treks to the Gulch.
All move off Stage L
SCENE 2
GARDEN AT BECKFOOT
IT IS LATE AFTERNOON. COOK AND BILLY ARE LOOKING UP, ANXIOUSLY.
Cook: *(twisting the hem of apron and sounding agitated)* Miss Turner! Miss Turner, is that you?
Dot: (*from Stage L)* Something's happened.
Cook: Eh, thank goodness you've come back. Isn't your aunt with you?
Nancy: Of course she isn't. We've been to High Topps. *(Pause, while Cook takes this in).*
Cook: She's gone.
Peggy: But where, when, how?
Cook: Nay, if I knew that, I wouldn't be in such a scrow. Two o'clock she was away, and Bill here was the last to see her in this world . . .
Tim: *(appearing, somewhat out of breath)* But what's all

THE GA RETURNS AND LEAVES

this?
Billy: *(scratching his head)* It's me to blame, forgetting about looking in tank, what with Miss Turner waiting to be off.
Nancy: But <u>off where</u>? What happened?
Cook: She had her lunch. And then she sent me for Billy to drive the car for her. Stiff as a poker she was, and waiting with her blue parasol and all . . . little I thought I'd never see her again.
Tim: But where was she going? Billy must know where he took her!
Billy: She told me to take t'lake road and go along for Swainson's. . . We'd not gone above a mile likely when the engine went funny, and then it stopped, and what with her asking questions and all, I was a bit before I found what was gone with it. Tank was empty. And she sent me running back to fetch some petrol, and there wasn't a drop in the garage.
Nancy: Bother the petrol! Where did you take her?
Billy: I come back, and there was t'owd car where I'd left it at t'side o't'road and nobody in it. – She was gone.
Tim: *(quietly and deliberately)* What did you do?
(Nancy looks across at Tim respectfully, as he appears to take charge)
Billy: I didn't do nowt. I emped the petrol in, and I sat there waiting for her. I thought: maybe she'd gone for a walk.
Tim: What was that place she mentioned?
Billy: Swainson's farm.
Tim: Did you go and ask there?

Billy: Nay, I'd turned back before that.
Tim: We'll go there now.
Cook: You'll not find her at Swainsons. Loss of memory, that's what it is. Wandering on t'fells likely enough. <u>And dark coming on.</u>
Nancy: *(glancing anxiously at Dot and Peggy).* Shut up Cook!
Cook: I've a feeling in my bones.
ALL LEAVE STAGE – NANCY, TIM, BILLY TO RIGHT – COOK, PEGGY AND Ds TO LEFT.
SCENE 3
SCULLERY AT BECKFOOT
COOK IS HOLDING A LARGE, BLACK SAUCEPAN, WHILST PREPARING SUPPER; THE Ds ARE KNEELING ON A BENCH AND WATCHING OUT OF THE WINDOW.
Cook starts as car horn is heard, and nearly drops the pan.
Cook: *(to Dick and Dorothea, who have scattered, looking for somewhere to hide)* Now, you bide still. They'll stop at the front door if they've found her.....Nay, I <u>knew</u> they hadn't.
Nancy: *(entering brusquely, closely followed by Tim)* She's not been to Swainson's.
Dot: You don't think she's found out about us and gone off in a rage?
Nancy: *(exasperated) If* she <u>wanted</u> to vanish, she might have waited another two days. If she disappeared at <u>Harrogate</u>, people would simply say "Three Cheers" or "R.I.P.", and have a celebration. But disappearing here! When we've kept her happy all the time, and only one day to go before she clears out properly . . . Oh, Giminy,

THE GA RETURNS AND LEAVES

Giminy, what will Mother say?
Tim: She'll turn up all right.
Dick: She might have tumbled in the lake.
Cook: Ay, they'll drag for her . . .
Tim: *(hastily changing the subject)* She may have sat down and fallen asleep.
Nancy: *(helpfully)* She always did sleep in the afternoon.
Tim: . . . But if she doesn't walk in soon, I'll have to telephone to the Police . . . We'll have to have a regular search, and the more men they can send the better!
Nancy: *(excitedly)* There's Colonel Jolys! I'll go and ring him up at once. He'll be delighted at the chance of <u>really doing something</u>.

SCENE 4
RIDGE OVERLOOKING BECKFOOT
DICK AND DOT WATCH FROM THE HILL AS PREPARATIONS FOR THE SEARCH BEGIN.
Jacky, appearing from Stage R, carrying a milk can.
Jacky: *(panting)* Have you heard what's oop? You should be down at Beckfoot. They've the firefighters and the Police and all. Sergeant's brought his bloodhound. And my Dad's coming with our Bess. She's a right clever dog. There's owd Miss Turner done away wi' herself, that's what my mother says. They're going to hunt the woods for her, and if they don't find her they'll be dragging the lake. Eh, but I hope they'll let me go in the boat.
Dot: I'm sure she hasn't killed herself.
Jacky: That's what my Dad says. He says she'll have got herself cragfast or brambled like, so's she can't move,

same's a sheep.
Dot: Just laying and waiting to be found.
Jacky: Happen they'll find her, happen they won't. I'm off to see.
Dot: I'm not going any nearer.
A lot of noise is heard. The voice of COL JOLYS is heard off-stage
Col. Jolys: Now, men. We want one chap to every fifty yards. Ten to a team. We start at the lake shore, and work up the woods to the fell. Each team leader sounds his horn from time to time so that we can keep in touch and, the moment she's found, the nearest leader gives a single, long blast, as long as he can blow. Understand?
A long blast of the horn is heard. DOT puts fingers to ears.
Dick: There's Nancy - and look how she's dressed!
Dot: Yes, that's her best frock – to please the Great Aunt if they find her.
Dick: There's Timothy, just come out of the gate. He's talking to Col. Jolys. He's going too.
Dot: No he's not ... *(peers into distance)*. He's going to <u>our house</u>. Quick, we must stop him!.
Both exit L.
Enter TIM, R, looking around him.
Dick: *(from Wings, softly)* Hullo!
TIM stops - he looks very tired and dishevelled. Spots DICK who returns from L.
Tim: Good. No-one's seen you? I was just coming up to tell you what we think you'd better do, If we don't find her where we think she is, in the wood at the side of the road, those lads will be hunting here, there and everywhere,

THE GA RETURNS AND LEAVES

asking questions. You're best out of the way. Agreed?
Dot: Do you think Miss Turner's all right?
Tim: I'm sure she is – broken ankle perhaps – doctor says there's nothing wrong with her heart. That's what I was afraid of. . . .The main thing is, we've got to keep you out of her way.
Dot: But where can we go?
Tim: There's only one place where you'll be sure of meeting nobody. You can slip down to your boat now. They've all gone the other way. Wait for me on Jim's houseboat. Plenty of grub there. Take what you can put in a knapsack so that you can doss down if you have to. But <u>go now</u>.
Dick: All right then.
Tim: You see, the one thing that mustn't happen is for you to meet the old lady.

SCENE 5
LAWN AT BECKFOOT
CROWD HAS GATHERED AWAITING THE GREAT AUNT'S RETURN. *DICK'S voice is heard Offstage.*
Dick: I'll row now. Will you put the rowlocks ready.
Dot: Shall I lower the sail?
Dick: No need, we'll be on the port tack going up, and the wind will keep the sail out of the way.
Dot: Ready now.
Dick: Change places with me.
"View Halloos" are now heard Offstage.
Nancy: *(enters, shouting to overcome the tremendous noise hooting, barking, etc.)* It's all up. She's met the Picts. She's

<u>in the boat with them</u>. They're coming round the point now.
Peggy: What shall we do? Bolt?
Nancy: We can't. There'll be the most awful row. We've just got to explain.
Tim: *(suddenly appearing, mopping his brow)* Thank goodness she's found. Worse things might have happened.
Nancy: Nothing could be worse than that.
Tim: Dragging the lake! Come on, we've got to take what's coming to us.
Cook: *(comes out, running)* Have they found her? Is she badly hurt?
Nancy: Dick and Dot have found her. She's in their boat. They'll be here any minute now.
Cook: Them two! I knew all along it would come to that. *(Wringing her hands).* She'll find out all now – and what she'll say to your poor mother!
Doctor: *(advancing towards group). (To NANCY)* I ought to have given you away at once. Then this would never have happened.
(They turn towards back of stage, looking in direction crowd are facing).
Jacky: *(with a cry of complaint on seeing the G.A.).* They won't be dragging the lake after all.
Nancy: *(digging PEGGY sharply in the ribs).* You'd better leave the talking to me.
Peggy: *(in a stage whisper).* Where did they find her?
Nancy: <u>I</u> don't know! They were bringing her up the lake when I saw them first – half way between Long Island and our promontory. <u>Idiots</u> to go and pick her up if they saw

THE GA RETURNS AND LEAVES

her on the shore.
Peggy: When I last saw them, they were going the other way!
Tim: I told them that the one thing that mustn't happen was for them to meet her, and that they were to go to the houseboat and sit tight.
Nancy: Mutton-headed galoots! If only they'd done as they were told. . . . Hullo, here they are.

(Crowd surges forward, SCARAB emerges slowly from R.)
THE G.A. CAN BE HEARD SAYING: OFF STAGE
G.A.: If you will put me ashore here.
Dick: *(off stage)* I don't think she'll go into the boathouse with the mast up.
G.A.: I believe there is quite deep water at the edge of the lawn.
(People catch hold of SCARAB, and it is the Doctor who gives his hand to the G.A. to help her ashore. . . Crowd moves back a pace or two.
COL. JOLYS steps forward)
Peggy: She doesn't look as if anything had happened at all
Col. Jolys: Give her room to get ashore.
Peggy: He's pretty sick he didn't find her.
Nancy: He's had a good run for his money, anyhow.
(Col. Jolys gestures to his men to keep quiet).
Tim:*(turning to audience).* Bless my soul, he's going to make a speech.
Col. Jolys:*(clearing his throat).* Miss Turner, I think I am speaking for all of us when I say . . .
G.A.: Tommy Jolys, am I right in supposing that you're the leading spirit in this foolery?
(COL. JOLYS shifts about uncomfortably)
G.A.:*(continuing)* No, Tommy. You have changed very little. You always liked toy trumpets. . . I remember you howling with temper because your sister had trodden on the tin trumpet you had then. There you lay on the nursery floor, howling and kicking, until your mother picked you up and very properly chastised you.
Col. Jolys:*(as one of the firefighers stifles a giggle, and the*

audience laugh) M-M-Miss Turner

G.A.: Tin trumpets. Tommy.
Nancy: *(coming between COL. JOLYS and the POLICE SERGEANT).* Aunt Maria, are you all right? We've been in the most awful stew about you . . .
G.A.: *(walking forward, as bystanders give room).* Quite all right my dears – Do you know Ruth you've torn your frock? And Margaret seems to have been rolling on the grass in hers.
Cook: *(breaking in).* And how would they not, Miss Turner, hunting the woods looking for your 'corpus'. There's never a white frock made to last two minutes in them brambles.

G.A.: Ah, Cook, it is nearly one o'clock when, as I think you know, I shall be going to the station. I hope you have remembered to prepare my sandwiches.
Cook: Sandwiches, Miss Turner? We was thinking more likely you were gone where you wouldn't need sandwiches.
G.A.: *(stiffly)* I hope they will be ready.
Sergeant: It is Miss Turner, isn't it? We were informed last night that you had disappeared, leaving no trace, from a motor car left standing on the road ...
G.A.: I am not, as far as I know, under any obligation to keep the police informed of my whereabouts. Nor, if you will allow me to say so, have I any reason to suppose them other than disgracefully incompetent.
Sergeant: *(making an effort to keep his cool)* I should point out to you. Miss Turner, that a section of the Police have been taken from their duties, and a large number of other men have had to leave their work . . .
Nancy: *(moving forward 'to the rescue')* She had nothing to do with it. It was just that Aunt Maria didn't come home. I got a bit worried and couldn't think of anything else to do, except for telephoning for you and Col. Jolys.
Col. Jolys: *(seizing his opportunity)* And, madam, I think I may say that, though we did not have the good fortune to find you, my men made a pretty good job of the search, if, by any chance you had fallen anywhere in these woods, I think one or other of us could hardly have failed to rescue you.
G.A.: *(scornfully, but quietly)* Tin trumpets. I hope at least you have enjoyed yourselves, even though you were looking for someone who was never lost.

THE GA RETURNS AND LEAVES

Sergeant: Madam, I have to complete my report. Have you any objection to stating where, in fact, you were?

G.A.: None whatsoever, Sergeant. I was in my nephew's houseboat, which I found unattended, and in a disgraceful condition.

(At this, surprise shows on the faces of NANCY, TIM, and PEGGY. TIM comes forward whilst SERGEANT OF POLICE writes busily in notebook.)

Tim: Miss Turner, I really must apologize. If I had known you were coming, I would have done a bit of tidying.

G.A.: *(looking Tim up and down, disapprovingly).* We have, I think, met before. Unwillingly on your part. If you remember, you jumped over a wall and ran away into the wood. ... I cannot say I congratulate my nephew on his choice of friends. As for the state in which I found his houseboat, to describe it as a pigsty is unjust to the brute creation. You will at least, when you go back there, be able to make a fresh start, and I hope you will try to keep it clean for the 24 hours before he returns... I have spent much of the morning emptying dirt into the lake. . . . And now, if you'll excuse me, I must leave you. Bad manners, are, alas, infectious, and *(starts to look round)* I have yet to thank the two charming and well-behaved children but for whose unselfish action I should have been in danger of missing my train.

ALL turn back towards river – surprised murmurs as they discover the Ds are not there.

Nancy: *(almost a shout of relief).* They've gone!

G.A.: I have been most remiss. . . I omitted to ask their names. *(to Nancy and Peggy)* I dare say you will see them

again on the lake. They would, I think, be most suitable friends for you. . . .Will you tell them that the old lady to whom they were so kind is very sorry she had no opportunity of saying how grateful she was? And now, the motor car I have ordered should be here at any minute.
(The G.A. makes as if to go into house, but Col. Jolys intervenes.)
Col. Jolys: Miss Turner, I have a car here, and if I may offer you a lift . . .
G.A.:*(starchily)* Thank you, Tommy, but your triumph must be incomplete. You have had your noisy hunt, but I fear you must go home without carrying your kill in your car. *(She spots the Constable carrying her cloak)* Constable, what are you doing with that cloak?
Constable: We had to have something, Miss, just to give the smell to the dog.
G.A.:*(draws breath)* Do you mean to say that you have had the impertinence to open my boxes? I packed that cloak yesterday.
Constable: W-we didn't t-touch owt else.
G.A.: Take it from him, Margaret.
Nancy:*(enjoying this)* It was for the bloodhound.
G.A.: I know . . . Bloodhound indeed! *(to Constable)* You are, I think, Mrs Lewthwaite's son? It would be useless to talk to your sergeant, but I regret that I am leaving too soon to have <u>a few words with your Mother.</u>
Col. Jolys:(As the *G.A. sweeps off)* Come on, men, Three Cheers for Miss Turner!
SCENE 6
A TRANQUIL BECKFOOT LAWN SOME TIME LATER

THE GA RETURNS AND LEAVES

DICK, DOROTHEA, NANCY, PEGGY, TIM, sitting, relaxing. COOK approaches.
Cook: You'll be staying to lunch, Mr Stedding? I'm laying for five . . . Eh, but I'm glad that's over. And to think of Miss Turner spending the night in yon old boat, as comfortable as you please, with us thinking of inquests and all.
Nancy: She's written to Mother to say we've been awfully good. But, I say, Cooky, you aren't <u>really going to leave?</u>
Cook: Oh <u>that</u>! She asked me to take my notice back and I was that pleased to see her alive I told her I didn't mind if I did. And now, lunch'll be ready as soon as I ring the gong, and you come in sharp. *(Puts an arm on shoulder of each of the Ds)* You've everything to bring down from that old ruin – we must have them back in their bedrooms like Christians again, ready for Mrs Blackett coming home. We must have everything just right. And so it would have been if Miss Turner'd left well alone.
(Turns and exits R)
There is a pause of sighs (and yawns,) . NANCY hums a line or two of John Peel. Then Timothy speaks:
Tim: *(leaning back in deckchair)* Thank goodness that's over!
Nancy: Yes, and only ten days gone after all. An awful ten days, but worth it to save Mother. And now, at least we're free to start stirring things up. We'll hoist the skull and crossbones again the moment we've had our grub. We'll get things moving without wasting a minute . . .
Tim: *(sitting up)* Oh look here! I'm all for a quiet life after this.

Nancy: Well, you won't exactly have one. Not yet. You can't expect it. Not with the Swallows coming, and Uncle Jim – and five whole weeks of the holiday still to go.
Three Million Cheers!
ALL cheer. PEGGY waves the Skull and Crossbones and the Ds flourish the Scarab flag.

The music John Peel plays, and the set darkens.

Mrs Blackett: (*re-enters*) Well! That all just before I got home; and once my home-coming was over, the children certainly didn't waste those five weeks. The Walkers came surging in and there was lots of camping on Wild C6at Island, and Dick and Dorothea got on really well with their sailing in *Scarab* – in their different ways! – but they're terrific sailors now. Then

THE GA RETURNS AND LEAVES

Timothy was able to retreat on to the houseboat and into the mine as Jim got back into the copper-working, and we all got back to normal.

I think the next drama was when all the children were up here, and busy sailing the lake, and of all the astonishing things they bumped into three young lads from Norfolk – the Death and Glories – who Dick and Dorothea had got to know when they were on holiday down there. Some of it got written up in an account called 'Coots in the North'; it was a wonderful summer, with the children sailing and fishing, and Professor Callum – Dick and Dorothea's father – coming up and being taught to sail; and the drama of the summer was when Jim's houseboat broke her moorings in a gale and the Death and Glories sprang into action and saved her from drifting on to the rocks.

After that – well, the children were growing up, but they did have a last terrific adventure, when Jim heroically took them all off to the Hebrides for a voyage and they ended up doing all sorts of dramatic things about birds and Scots but – well, justifying my faith in them all by showing how they were all becoming useful to the world. It's a tale to be told!

So I'll finish. I do hope you've enjoyed this entertainment, and all of us would specially like to thank the playwright Gill Gordon and our beloved producer, Brian Hopton. Thank you!

RANSOME CENTRE STAGE

AUSTARS

THE RADIO PLAYS

by

Jan Allen

AusTars indoor meetings are usually held in a member's home. These plays are therefore intended for low-key performance among friends, and keep closely to the books. Audience participation is encouraged. However, you will notice that sound effects and music play a great part in the action.

These 'radio plays' appear in what might be called 'the wrong order', but that is because the *Great Northern?* version has a fuller explanation of how they were done. They are obviously intended for intimate winter meetings when it's "dark at teatime, and nothing ever happens." Not true when AusTars are around!

GREAT NORTHERN?

A Musical Play for TARS by Janet Allen

(courtesy of AR)

Method:	Divide the company into three groups. Each group has an act to perform. They prepare these separately.
	ALL sing the prologue and finale songs.
	The groups act the scenes as listed for their act of the play, either in 'mime' or 'voiced', and intersperse the action with the appropriate songs.
	The idea is for everyone in the group to be involved and entertained.
Accompaniment:	Could be a tin whistle/accordion, whatever the available talent can muster.
Sound Effects:	Can be added. Players could walk across 'stage' carrying placard depicting the scene or compère can introduce the play and its setting.
Setting:	An (unnamed) island in the Outer Hebrides.
Period:	Mid-20th century.

RANSOME CENTRE STAGE

Characters: The captain and crew of the *Sea Bear*. Swallows, Amazons, Ds, Captain Flint.
'Young chieftain', old chieftain, ghillies, Gaels
Mr. Jemmerling and sailor from *Pterodactyl*

Regrettably, no photo of the production, but here are AusTars on a Viking Day. Perhaps they thought the Gaels had Viking ancestors?
(L-R: Nancy Endersby-Harshman, Bradley Spiers, Jessica Spiers, Alison Spiers, Martin Spiers, Larry Harshman)

AUSTARS – GREAT NORTHERN?

	Prologue
ALL	**Tune: Over the Sea to Skye**

Chorus:	Speed, bonnie boat, like a bird on the wing
Over the sea to Skye
A voyage 'round Scotland has been just the thing
Off to the islands we'll fly.

Verse:	High on a cliff
A watcher there stands
Young chieftain of his clan
On the *Sea Bear*
Dick dreams of birds
Will any divers be there?

Chorus:	Speed, bonnie boat, like a bird on the wing
Over the sea to Skye
A voyage 'round Scotland has been just the thing
Off to the islands we'll fly.

ACT ONE
Scene 1:	**Off to island for last day of cruise.**
Scene 2:	**Dick's discovery.**
Scene 3:	**Proof – but the birdman is the enemy and follows!**

Song 1	**Tune:	My Bonnie lies over the Ocean**
Verse 1	The elders are scrubbing the *Sea Bear*
And we are all free to explore
Roger has found a strange lair
Let's go up the glen to see more.

Chorus:	'Go back, go back!' We certainly startled the grouse

                    But Dick has gone down to the lochs
                    The Gaels are around, but what has Dick found
                    While hidden down there in the rocks?
Verse 2:   Something is definitely wrong
                    We'd better be getting along
                    The Gaels are upset, that's for sure
                    Quick, back to the ship once more.

L-R: Alison Spiers, Bradley Spiers, Nancy Endersby-Harshman and Jan Allen in chorus

Song 2   **Tune: Drunken Sailor**
                    What shall we do about the evil egg man?
                    How can we stop him following our Dick?
                    We need to have a pretty good plan
                    To save those eggs, we'll have to be quick!

AUSTARS – GREAT NORTHERN?

ACT TWO
Scene 1: The plan is made for photographic proof.
Scene 2: The decoys' plan fails and they are captured by unfriendly natives.
Scene 3: But Jemmerling finds the loch!

Song 1   **Tune: D'ye ken John Peel?**
D'ye ken those Gaels, they're following us
Wherever we walk, through the heather they stalk
It's not just that sailor we've got to avoid
We've stirred up the locals, and they seem annoyed

Song 2   **Tune: Botany Bay**
Oh, we're trapped now and captured by Gaels
Just when we thought Dick was all clear
Locked u-up, wind gone from our sai-ails
And only Roger can help – if he's near.

Chorus: Oh the mission has now got all mixed up
And it's not just a storm in a tea cup
If we can't make those Gaels understand
Our divers will be gone from Scotland.

ACT THREE
Scene 1: The Gaels finally understand the situation.
Scene 2: But Jemmerling has taken the eggs. He's caught, but the sailor escapes with the eggs.
Scene 3: Can they catch him in time?

Song 1   **Tune: Blow The Man Down**
Hunt the man down, hearties,
Let's find him, quick
Way hay, hunt the man down!

Chase him and catch him
Those eggs he shan't nick
Way hay, hunt the man down!

Song 2   **Tune: Will Ye No' Come Back Again?**
All has ended well at last
The divers are back on their nest
Jemmerling's in gaol, held fast
Thanks to Dick, who did his best

Islanders now thank Sea Bears
For the divers have no cares
Sea Bear sailors welcome, then!
Will ye no' come back again?

ALL SING FINALE SONG

Song 3   **Tune: Spanish Ladies (extend vowels for scansion)**
Finale:
Farewell and adieu to you gallant Sea Bears
Farewell and adieu, hope to see you once more
May your voyage be calm and your weather be fair
The Great Northern Divers are safe now, all four!

FINIS

Verses © J.E. Allen

MISSEE LEE

for a group of TARS

Songs to accompany the acting of appropriate scenes

by Janet Allen

Song 1:   Sung to the tune of the chorus of 'Waltzing Matilda'.

Song 2:   Sung to 'The Quartermaster's Store'.

Song 3:   Sung to the tune of 'Botany Bay'.

Song 4:   Sung to the tune of 'Drunken Sailor'.

SONG 1
Chorus of 'Waltzing Matilda'

Sailing to China, sailing to China,
Who'll come a-sailing to China with us?
Though the *Wild Cat's* gone, we're all saved and the sextant too
Who'll come a-sailing to Lee, Chang and Wu?

SONG 2

Verse of 'The Quartermaster's Store'

All: There was rice, rice, nothing else to eat
                              In the cage, in the cage
                              There was rice, rice, never something nice
                              In the cage of Taicoon Chang

Captain Flint: This bed's so-o hard, it hurts my hip
                              I cannot ever get some kip
                              My heart it i-is so sad,
                              For I have lost my ship

All: *Repeat both verses above.*

SONG 3

Chorus of 'Botany Bay' (Toorali . . .)

Sing we – learning our Latin is so much fun (ha! ha!)
We-ee won't ever want to go home
But declensions and grammar will soon be done
We'll be off in a junk o'er the foam

SONG 4

Finale

Tune: 'Drunken Sailor'

Verse: Don't you get caught by that Missee Lee-ee
              Queen of the China Sea is she-ee
              Missee Lee! No pirate's finer
              She's the boss in China

Chorus: Hoo-ray for the pirate quee-een
              Toughest lady you've ever see-een
              Missee Lee! No pirate's finer
              She's the boss in China

©J.E. Allan

Something more ambitious now – a whole book in six songs.

WINTER HOLIDAY – THE MUSICAL
To be performed informally by a small group of Tars as cast, to an audience of other Tars in a home environment.

To be accompanied by suitable gestures. Props as available.

Scene One:
Dick & Dot. Chorus sings first verse
Tune: Oh what a beautiful morning.

All: Up at the lake for the winter
Visitors for the first time.
Dick wants to look at the night sky,
Dot dreams of stories and rhyme.

Dick: Oh what a fine frosty morning,
Silas said soon there'll be ice.
Even the lake might freeze over,
Skating up here will be nice.

Dot: Look! On the lake there's a rowboat!
Just children who make up its crew.
That small one has put on his warm coat –
Now what are they going to do?

Dick: Let's climb the fell to that old barn.
There's plenty of sky from up there.
By day we can see to that far farm,
At night I will see the Great Bear.

Dot: Those children rowed off to that island.

AUSTARS – WINTER HOLIDAY

      They seemed to be having such fun
      Waving their flags for a message.
      We don't understand what they've done.
           [*murmurs:* The Outcasts]

Dick: We know now they come from that farmhouse.
      We earthlings could signal to Mars.
      Tonight we can try with the lantern
      When we go up to look at the stars.

Both *[spoken]*: Yes! Let's try signalling to Mars.

<u>Scene Two</u>:
Ds, Swallows and Peggy (and Nancy verses 1 & 2)
Tune: My Bonnie lies over the ocean.

Dick & Dot: Our flashes went out through the dark night
      The Martians in turn flashed their light.
      Now we're helping them cover the igloo
      And we Ds are part of the crew.

Swallows: Nancy has plans for the Arctic,
      A crossing right up to the North.
      We'll conquer that vast sheet of sea-ice,
      Explorers will soo-oon set forth!

PAUSE

All: Oh no, oh woe,
      We've lost our great leader so fast, what now?
      She's lumpy, she's mumpy,
      In bed with a big fat red face – wow!

Peggy: But wait! Maybe all is not lost yet,
      Even if Nancy's the cost.
      A month's holiday has come our way.
      We could <u>all</u> reach that Arctic yet one day!

RANSOME CENTRE STAGE

L-R: Hedley Thomson, Jan Allen, Alison Spiers and Nancy Endersby-Harshman

<u>Scene Three</u>:
All except Nancy
Tune: Frère Jacques

Roger, Titty & Dot:
    Look! a fur heap there!
    It's a sheep! Where?
    On that ledge
    Below the cliff edge

        Dick can rescue <u>that</u> sheep
    From an endless <u>death</u> sleep
    He has a plan
    And do it he can.

AUSTARS – WINTER HOLIDAY

          Dick has rope now,
Can he cope – how?
Bum on the ledge,
Right on the edge.
Save the polar bear, Dick!
Get the rope around, quick!
Don't look down.
Don't look down.   Will the rope give?
Will the sheep live?
Dick is numb.

All: But John has come!
He's got the dogs all helping,
There'll be no panicked yelping
Both safe down.
Both safe down.

Scene Four
All

Tune: "Ode to Joy" Beethoven's 9th symphony final movement theme – first two lines and repeat.

All: Rescued polar bear's alive but Dick is not the one to brag
Mr Dixon is impressed by courage shown upon that crag.
He knows just how to thank Dick for going on that narrow ledge.
He and Silas worked that night, and now the Ds have their own sledge.

Scene Five
All

Tune: I'm getting married in the morning

All: We're doing all that Nancy told us:
Spitzbergen, Greenland, Nansen's ship.
It's still our go-oal

RANSOME CENTRE STAGE

To reach the Po-ole
Perhaps we <u>all</u> will skate on that trip!

      We know that Nancy's out of bed now.
Soon she'll be training on the ice.
Meanwhile the Fra-am
Is all out of ja-am.
Those stores have made the great sacrifice!

L-R: Elizabeth Stamp, Alison Spiers, Jan Allen, Bradley Spiers, Nancy Endersby-Harshman, Hedley Thomson, with paper Winter Holiday creations. Hedley is blowing the ice yacht along.

AUSTARS – WINTER HOLIDAY

FINALE
Tune: Jingle Bells

All:
[Chorus tune]
>We're all here
>At the Pole
>Made it all the way!
>Ds are safe
>So it's all right
>Even though it's ni-ight.

>Oh – Arctic trek
>What the heck
>We have all got here.
>Never mind the wind and snow
>To the Pole we'd go.

[Verse tune]
>Dashing through the night
>What's the poor Ds' plight?
>Nancy has to go
>After all that snow

>Swallows follow on
>They are worried too.
>Captain Flint and Molly must
>O'er the ice they flew.

[Chorus tune]
>At the Pole,
>At the Pole,
>Expedition's here.
>Safe and sound,
>Grub around.
>Let's all give a cheer!
>Hoorah!

RANSOME CENTRE STAGE

And finally, AusTars produced a 'radio play' without music: one of our favourite most dramatic scenes.

ALL AT SEA

A Play by Arthur Ransome arranged for radio by Janet Allen

FX: Gentle slap of water against boat hull – continues behind voices.
Clang! *(loud bell sounds)*

Susan: John! John! It's here!

FX: Clang!
Roger: It's coming jolly fast!

Titty: It's going to bunt into us!

FX: Clang!
Susan: Oh, John! That was the Beach End buoy. We're out at sea! Drifting in the fog!

Music:

Roger: Susan's in a stew.

Titty: They both are, rather.

Roger: She's quite bobby about.

Titty: ... Yes

Susan: (*desperate*) We promised we wouldn't go outside the harbour.

AUSTARS – ALL AT SEA

John: We didn't mean to. Come on, Susan. Do help.

Roger: (*whispers*) Susan's going to cry.

Titty: Look the other way.

Roger: What do you think they'll do?

Music: (to fade)

John: Hi, Titty! Take turns with the foghorn.

FX: *Lightship foghorn "Bee-uu" (distantly).*
John: Hoot for all you're worth if you hear anyone else hooting.

Susan: *(shrieks)* John! There's another buoy!

Titty: It's going to hit us!

Susan: John! John!

Roger: Gosh! That was close.

Susan: Oh, John!

John: We can't go on drifting. We can't steer. I've got to get some sail on her.

Susan: But do you know how?

John: I think so. I'm sure I can get the mainsail up somehow. And the jib's only rolled up.

Roger: Can I come and help?

Susan: Sit still.

Music: (brief)

Susan: Come and take her. I don't know which way to go.

John: Look out of the way, Roger. Let her pay off, Susan.

More. Quick. We're heading straight for the shoals along the shore!

Susan: John, if you're sure the land's over there, why not go straight for it and get ashore somehow?

John: We can't. We'd only wreck the *Goblin*. And already we've lost his anchor.

Susan: But we ought.

John: *(almost angrily)* We can't. Go and look at the chart. There are rocks even so far out from shore and in the fog we wouldn't know which way to swim.

FX: Bee-uu (long wail of siren).
Susan: Mother'd be wanting us to try.

John: I don't believe she would. . . And Daddy wouldn't anyway. Look here, Susan. We're all right in *Goblin*. We've only got to keep clear of things. The fog can't last for ever. Keep a lookout for anything you can see. Anything. . .

FX: (siren wailing distantly)
Roger: How many hoots do I give?

Titty: *(faintly)* Three hoots. Sailing vessel with the wind aft. Remember Peter Duck.

FX/Roger: (sounds foghorn) It's a real bull-roarer.

FX: (sounds it twice more)
John: We've got to get outside the shoals. Look at the chart for yourself.

Susan: But we can't. We can't.

FX: (foghorn blares)
Susan: Oh, shut up, Roger!

Roger: I must do it twice more.   Otherwise they'll think we're close-hauled.

Susan: *(angrily)*   Who'd think?

Roger: *(shouts as blares horn)*   Anyone who hears it.

FX: *(increasing sounds of wind and waves – continuing)*
John: We must be getting near the lightship.

Susan: *(moans)* But we promised not to go to sea at all…

John: We didn't do it on purpose. We're at sea now, and we can't get back in the fog.

Titty: We can't keep a promise if it's already broken.

Susan: How shall we ever get back?

John: Susan, I know it's all right.

   (short silence)

Titty: I'm awfully sorry.   I. . . I think I'm going to be sick.

John: Nobody's going to be sick.

Susan: It's all wrong!   We must go back.   I didn't want to, and I can't bear it.

John: We can't go back.   It isn't safe to try.

Susan: *(crying)*   We must!

FX: *(sound of retching)*
Roger: She's being sick.

Titty: Leave me alone.   I can't be.   I'll be all right if I lie down just for a minute.

Susan: *(furiously)*   I'm going to help her.

FX: *(noises as they go down into the cabin)*

RANSOME CENTRE STAGE

Susan: Try to go to sleep. *(moans)* Oh, oh.

FX: (scrambling sounds then retching sounds)
John: Susan. Poor old chap.

John: Susan. We've simply got to sound the foghorn.

Susan: *(sobs)*

FX: (foghorn sounds 3 times) Fade.
John: Fog's lifting at last. With this wind I thought it was bound to blow away.

Roger: It's going.

John: There's something else coming.

Roger: What is it?

John: Rain.

Roger: *(cheerfully)* The wind came first. Remember Daddy's rhyme?

    'When the wind's before the rain,
    Soon you may make sail again.'

John: Hallo! Listen. Can you hear anything?

FX: (2 long blasts and a short one)
John: That's another lightship. It's a long way off.

Susan: John, aren't we going to turn back?

John: Look what's coming up... It's no good turning just now.

FX: (rain drops patter hard)
John: Oilskins. Quick.

Susan: I can't go down.

AUSTARS – ALL AT SEA

John: Take the tiller. No, look out. This is a tough one.

FX: (rising wind and rain)
John: Good man, Roger.

FX: (heavier rain and wilder wind) (fade to short silence) (music to fade)

FX: (wind and wavesounds)
Roger: It's stopped raining.

Susan: Let's turn back now.

John: All right. I'll bring her round now. We'll have to haul in the mainsheet as she comes round. Sing out as soon as you're ready.

Susan: Ready now. The sooner the better. . .

FX: (sounds of water slamming and crashing noises)
John: Put the tiller down!

Susan: Stop it John! Stop it! I can't . . Oh, ough.

FX: (retching sounds)
Titty: Are we sinking? There's water on the floor of the cabin. I was thrown right out of my bunk.

John: It's all right. We got some water over when we tried to go the other way.

Susan: *(moans)* Oh. . . Oh.

John: We've got to get all that water out before we have another shot at turning back.

Susan: Oh, not again. I can bear it all right like this but it's too awful going the other way.

Roger: If Susan's going to pump the water, I'd better go down and help Titty in the cabin.

Susan: *(angrily)* Don't you feel sea-sick at all?

Roger: Not a bit.

Susan: Oh! Oh. . . Where's the handle, then?

FX: *(pump 3 times and stops)*
Susan: Oh. Sorry. John, I really am better. Four, five.

John: Count your strokes. You'll be all right.

Susan: Six. Seven.

Roger: Just shout if I'm wanted on deck.

Titty: I'm all right now, I think. I was asleep before I got flung out. What happened?

Roger: We tried turning round but it didn't work. So we're going on. . . But it's Susan herself who wants to go on now.

FX: *(music up to crescendo)*

FINIS

SCOTTISH REGION
Kirstie Taylor

Scottish region have a long tradition of 'Literary Days', and also presented some occasional 'duologues'. Only one survives, from Arthur's Birthday Party at Ellersley House Hotel, Edinburgh, on January 19th, 2013. It was performed by Kirstie Taylor, the author, as Evgenia, with Andrew Jones as Arthur.

Kirstie comments, "All the artefacts mentioned were produced in performance. Yes, that is a <u>real</u> fur coat wrapped round me – a library colleague gave it to use for Baloo in my *Jungle Book* display, and didn't want it back, as 'It's too heavy, dear.' I'll say it was!"

RANSOME CENTRE STAGE

JANUARY 18TH 1918

A Room in the Smolny Institute, Petrograd

[*Knock at the door. Arthur Ransome enters the room where Evgenia is sitting with a bowl of soup*]

AR   Hello there! What are you doing here? I thought you and Rosa were settled for the day over at the Foreign Office.

E   [*putting down the bowl*]
'Ello again, Artur. 'Appy Name Day!

AR   I keep telling you – it's my *birthday*. I'm English,

SCOTTISH REGION – SMOLNY INSTITUTE

I don't celebrate my Saint's Day....come to that, I never *heard* of a Saint Arthur ....only a *King* Arthur.

E None of your aristocratic heroes here, zis is Revolutionary Russia and if you are royal you have even *more* chance of being shot. Dosvodanya, Tzar Artur ....[*she points her finger and shoots*] PEW!

AR Steady on! Jolly good job your finger's not loaded like the real pistol. I don't want any holes in *me*....like the hole in the window....or the hole in the wall ....or....

E The vindow vos Trotsky, and be careful, I could do viz some target practice.

AR Way things are going we could all be targets tomorrow.

E 'Ow about ze Constituent Assembly? 'As anyone been shot zere or has it been as boring as Rosa Radek said it vould be?

AR Not even started yet, and I think it'll be a long night so I trotted over here to see if there was any soup left.

E [*sighs, wipes the spoon and hands him it and the bowl*] Zere you are. I can go down to ze Refectory again later.

AR Oh, thanks – gosh, I'm hungry. What would we do without potato soup?

E Starve.

AR [*noisily slurping the soup*]
What about you? I thought you and Rosa wouldn't leave that fire we got going for you. Not in this weather.

E	It may be vinter but for some of us it is not a 'oliday. Viz Trotsky away zere is a lot to be done and few able to do it. Besides, I had nozzing to read but zose Fairy Tales you lent me, and I vos getting annoyed viz zem ....zat Little Mermaid! Pah! Vot a ninny! Ze Robber Maid in 'Ze Snow Qveen' is the only von who 'as some ....oomph!
AR	What's the difference between a Robber Maid and a Revolutionary Maid?
E	Von 'as a dagger and money. Ze ozzer has a pistol and principles – but zey are boz dangerous to property-owning capitalists. Speaking of property ....here are your *Name* Day presents: [*flourishes them so the audience can see*] a new children's book, some cheese and a bear – a *Russian* bear.
AR	Oh, well done! Thanks ever so – I say, what a jolly fellow! He can join the rest of the menagerie on my typewriter table. [*He makes the bear dance.*]
E	Along viz the pictures of your home – your *English* home viz your hills and your lakes ....and your English vife. Vot vos the song Bruce Lockhart sang at 'is farevell party ven he got oh-so drunk and oh-so Scottish? *"Go back to your vife across ze sea, laddie. Go back to your bairnie..."*
AR	That's not fair. I've never lied to you. You know I'm married – unhappily married, and doing my best to escape Wiltshire.
E	Sorry. And, after all Bruce Lockhart 'ad *'is* vife viz 'im, and it certainly didn't stop *him! Men!* 'Ave you heard from her?

SCOTTISH REGION – SMOLNY INSTITUTE

AR   I haven't heard from anyone for *months,* not even Mother. It's not that they understand what's happening – or even understand Russia at all, but they do remind me there's a life outside this revolution... here it's so all-consuming, so exciting, so urgent that you get swept up in it, like in a waterspout. . .and then like the boom snapping over in a jibe, it all changes. People like Masefield (writer pal of mine) were so enthusiastic at the start because the old regime was so bally awful ....what did he say? It *"broke Dostoievsky, exiled Kropotkin, threatened Tolstoy, bullied Tchaikovsky"*....but what are they going to make of the Bolsheviks and *their* policies? ....Don't bristle!

E   It is nozzing to us vot zey make of us ...

AR   I know, I know, but it's so difficult for folk in England ....it's difficult enough for *us* and we're here in the middle of it all ....News from home gives me a chance to think of fishing and boats and important stuff like that – not trivial matters like revolutions. Then, of course I worry about my brother in France – Geoffrey's an absolute rotter, he never writes. [*He was already dead by then.*] And lately I've been dreaming about him. We keep setting off to walk to the Firth of Forth (that's the bit of sea near Edinburgh where he lived) and I keep losing him in a thick haar and ....

E   Vot is zis "haar"?

AR　　　　Sort of a sea-mist: very damp, very chilly, very clinging... very Scotch .... I'm yelling and all I can hear is bagpipes fading into the distance – he plays the bagpipes you know (doodlebags?) [*mimes playing them*]. Fearful noise really. Mother can't stand it, sends him up the nearest mountain to practise, but *he's* so jolly bucked at beating the Scots at their own damned tunes .... Mother's the one I feel sorriest for, just sitting at home while her children get into all sorts of dangerous situations .... I'm blethering on, amn't I? I'm tired and I'll have to concentrate on all the speeches – that's if Lenin doesn't close the Assembly down at gun-point – do *you* think he will?

E　　　　Zere is too much talk just now - and a lot of it

SCOTTISH REGION – SMOLNY INSTITUTE

dangerous. How do I know you're not an English spy?

AR   Do I *look* like a spy? The British think I'm a *Russian* spy, or at the very least a Red propagandist. Have we anything to go with the cheese?

E   Niet, ve're lucky to have zis - and save some for Eroida, she's coming over ven she finishes, and my sister is deadly ven she's hungry.

AR   Carve her bit off, then – save us from temptation – I must say I draw the line at Communism including birthday cheese. I wonder if I've time to get a telegram together for the *Daily News?*

E   Not if you're going to have a nosebleed as you usually do – anybody vould zink it vos 'ard vork. Does your body collapse ven you write fairy tales?

AR   No, of course not. Fairy tales are what I *want* to write, but I can't ignore a Revolution or a War when they're happening under my nose. How could I write children's stories and pretend a World War wasn't happening?

E   Qvite easily, I should zink. *You* read Hans Christian Andersen's *Fairy Tales* in the midst of war and revolution – vy should children not also vish to escape a reality zat includes bombs and hunger and corpses?

AR   Maybe you're right.

E   I'm *alvays* right.

AR   Of course you are – I'm only agreeing because I might need another pass for the Assembly tomorrow, you understand. *If* the Assembly meets

	tomorrow??
E	I told you zere is too much talk, not enough action.
AR	There were quite a few killed and more wounded today when those processions tried to reach the Tauride Palace – isn't that enough for you, you blood-thirsty revolutionary?
E	*Niet!* Zose people vere told to stay avay and still zey came. Ve should stop fighting each ozzer; stop ze var, stop ze hunger and zen, *only* zen, let ze endless talk, talk, talk begin. Ve have to vin ze Revolution first – and zat's not so certain yet. Ze Germans could come still and ve could all be dead tomorrow, so today let us live, let us laugh, let us ....how old *are* you today?
AR	34
E	Hah! An old man!
AR	None of your cheek! Just now I feel like a boy again. All this enthusiasm for a Brave New World...not that it'll happen without a fight though, both here and abroad. What I worry is that England will come in on the wrong side – there are so many reactionary Great-Auntish types there that disapprove of revolution or anything interesting and new. You know I'm not like that - no more squashy hats, only a soldier's cap will do.
E	You English! You zink var is a game – like chess. You play as long as you are interested or are vinning, zen you leave the mess behind and retreat to your safe island home.
AR	I know – a *little* island in a lake, overlooked by

SCOTTISH REGION – SMOLNY INSTITUTE

	North Country hills, just the place I'd like to retreat to....and the world and its politics could go hang.
E	And vot vould you do all day?
AR	Sail and fish and write stories.
E	Ach! Ze Fool of Ze Vorld!
AR	And look what happened to him – he married the Tzar's daughter and lived happily ever after.
E	Zat's a fairy tale as told by Old Peter ....or Old Artur...
AR	Not so much of the "old"! And what's wrong with "happily ever after"?
E	Nozzing. I'm just not sure zat it ever 'appens ....*except* in fairy tales. So, in your "happily ever after", say a hundred years from now, vot vill you be remembered for? Catching ze Vorld's Whopper Sturgeon? Vinning a sailing race? Or *children's* stories?
AR	*Yes!* Because 100 years from now, or "ever after", there will still be children. And wherever there are children – in Russia, in China, Caribbean islands, Holland, Ireland, Wales, in England or Scotland – children will *always* need stories ....and it's not only children who enjoy "children's" stories. We *all* need more "happily ever afters" in this world.
E	Hammers and Sickles! Vot an idealist!
AR	One can hope. [*heads for the door*] Meanwhile, back to the Revolution.
E	Dosvodanya, Tovarish.
AR	Goodbye, Comrade. [*he opens the door*]
E	Artur! [*he pauses and looks back*] 'Appy

RANSOME CENTRE STAGE

    Birzday!
[*AR laughs and exits*]
  E   The End.

BOHEMIA IN DURHAM

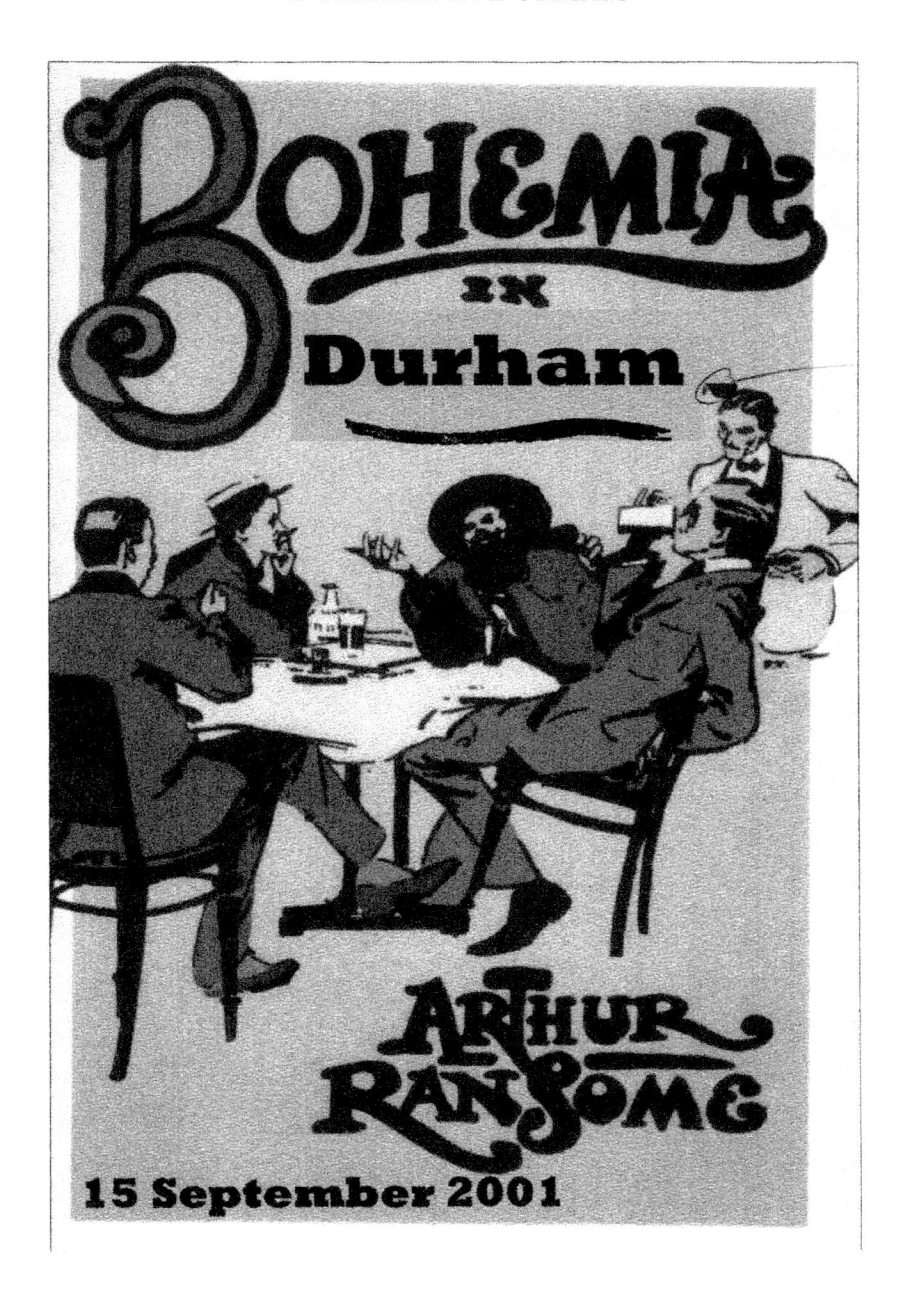

Arthur Ransome

15 September 2001

RANSOME CENTRE STAGE

Bohemia in London

In 1901, at the age of 17, the young Arthur Ransome arrived in London to seek fame and fortune in the literary world. Two years later, after a series of dead-end jobs, he had found himself a large empty room above a grocer's shop in Chelsea. In his *Autobiography* he tells us:

> In Chelsea I fell among friends and was extremely happy. ... I owed a great deal to Yoshio Markino, for taking me to the home of Miss Pamela Colman Smith in the Boltons. She was an artist who had been discovered in Jamaica ... by Ellen Terry. She had a weekly "evening" in her studio and I was soon one of the fortunate ones with a permanent invitation. Here I met for the first time W.B. Yeats ... He had given the name "purple hush" to the innocuous blend of claret and fizzy lemonade that we used to drink. Miss Nona Stewart ... used to sing the song of "Spanish Ladies" that had been written down in that very room, when Masefield heard a shy old sailor ... sing. Sooner or later would come the turn of the Anansi stories, which Pixie [Pamela] had heard as a child in Jamaica. ... I think I learned more of the art of narrative from those simple folk-tales than ever from any book.

Tonight we all participate in one of Pixie's Chelsea "evenings", as later recalled by Ransome, and as described by him at the time in the chapter "A Chelsea Evening" in *Bohemia in London* (1903). For this ambiance neither rum nor vodka but purple hush, or "opal hush" as it is described in *Bohemia in London*, will be served in abundance.

The Performers

Gabriel Woolf plays the part of the young Arthur Ransome. Well known for his many appearances in radio dramas, he has issued a series of tapes of readings of some of AR's books.

Flo Galbraith, who plays the part of the Stately Scottish Lady, is in real life the Chairman of TARS Scotland and a well-known singer and musician in Scotland.

Robert Thompson, who plays the part of the Actor, is an accomplished musician and singer. He is choirmaster at Ripon Cathedral and is a member of the chorus of Opera North. He is Junior Co-ordinator for Northern TARS.

Jane Grell is an accomplished story teller, specializing in the Anansi stories much loved by AR, which were a feature of Pixie Colman Smith's evenings. Jane is a teacher and lives in London.

Alan Hakim, who plays the part of the Japanese Gentleman, is TARS National Treasurer. He has visited Japan and members of the Arthur Ransome Club of Japan many times. During these visits, he has acquired a profound knowledge of that country and in this performance he will demonstrate a well-founded inscrutability ...

Extracts from *Bohemia in London*

Wilton, the actor, was happy. He thought he had a proselyte in me, and he talked like a prophet, till I wondered how it could be possible for any one man's brain to invent such floods of nonsense. I was happy under it all, if only on account of the quiet quizzical smile of the Japanese. The end of it was that he fell in love with an audience so silent, so appreciative, and decided that he must really have me with him that night, at the house of a lady who once a week gave an open party for her friends. I was wanted, it was clear, as a foil to his brilliance.

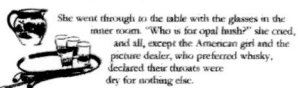

She went through to the inner room with the glasses in the inner room. "Who is for opal hush?" she cried, and all, except the American girl and the picture dealer, who preferred whisky, declared their throats were dry for nothing else.

Gypsy had spent some part of her life in the Indies, and knew a number of the old folk tales, of Annansee the spider, another Brer Rabbit in his cunning and shrewdness, and Chim Chim the little bird, and the singing turtle, and the Obeah Woman, who was a witch, "wid wrinkles deep as ditches on her old brown face." She told them in the old dialect, in a manner of her own. ... To hear her was to be carried back to the primitive days of story-telling.

TARS LITERARY WEEKEND 2001
Organising Committee
Robin Anderson (Chairman),
Ann Parr, Kirsty Nichol
Findlay, Alan Hakim, Geraint
and Helen Lewis, Kirstie
Taylor and Joy Wotton

142

Although Brian Hopton wrote plays for IAGMs, he never did one for the Literary Weekends. In fact, there were several professional productions over the years, but only one home-grown: *Bohemia in Durham*, produced by Robin Anderson and Kirsty Nichol Findlay, and derived from Arthur's first really successful book, *Bohemia in London*, published in 1907.

Sadly, it seems there was never a complete script, and all the principal players claim to have forgotten everything. Only one part survives, mine, as the Japanese poet, but there are plenty of photographs. There is also the report made by Malcolm Morrison for the *Transactions* of the weekend. It gives an excellent impression of the evening, and reveals some secrets of the 'Opal Hush' that accompanied it.

BOHEMIA IN DURHAM

SATURDAY 15 SEPTEMBER 2001

A REVIEW BY *MALCOLM MORRISON*

Imagine, if you will, a sitting room at the start of the last century. To be precise we are in the year 1903. Present in the room are a Japanese gentleman and an actor. The latter is lounging languishingly on a chaise longue with a cigarette louchly dangling from his long fingers. He is observed frequently to turn and glance into a mirror and preen: an action he achieves without moving from his recumbent position.
A visitor enters. A friendly looking young man wearing a soft

hat and smoking a pipe. This visitor, we soon learn is Arthur Ransome, who has recently moved into lodgings in the Chelsea district of London. He is paying a visit to friends he has newly acquired "through circumstances so typical of the snowball growth of acquaintances".

On AR's arrival the company resume their somewhat comic exchange on the art of dramatic characterisation, on which the

actor holds such brilliantly logical views that he will not hear of dissent. In this banter AR is happy to concur, tongue in cheek, to the actor's great authority.

The actor, perceiving that AR is a new acolyte to show off, suggests that they move on to the house of a lady known simply as 'Gypsy', where AR would "meet the best poets and painters and men and women of spirit in town"; a house where the actor himself goes regularly.

BOHEMIA IN DURHAM

The action moves on to Gypsy's house. Here, most wonderful musical delights were presented for the assembled company of friends. Firstly, the actor singing remarkably finely to his own piano accompaniment; to be followed by a "tall dark Scottish girl with a small head and beautiful graceful neck, very straight and splendid", whom AR calls "the princess". Accompanying herself on the harp, her repertoire included "the best of all the songs that have come to London from the sea'" – a song all Tars associate with AR – *Spanish Ladies*.

After the songs, story telling. We were treated to a number of old West Indian folk-tales of Annansee the spider, presented so intimately that the large auditorium shrank in size to the intimacy of an Edwardian drawing room, the audience becoming a part of the company assembled in Gypsy's "mad rooms".

And after the stories, the stately Scottish lady regaled the company with wistful songs of yearning for the Western Isles, including the Eriskay Love Lilt.

"Think of cloud on Bheinn na Cailleach,
Jagged Cuiffin soaring high,
Scent of peat and all the magic
Of the misty Isle of Skye!"

Then, all too soon, it was time for the audience to fast-forward and return to the 21st century.

BOHEMIA IN DURHAM

Bohemia in London was written by by the young AR to give "an impression of the untidy life" for young artists and writers seeking "the gold of fame on London pavements". For a brief time – a far too brief time – on this Saturday evening we had the privilege of returning to this earlier era when entertainment was self-made.

Kirsty Nichol Findlay and Robin Anderson have achieved a remarkable success not only in dramatising AR's writings but also, through imaginative staging, recreating the spirit of the Chelsea Evening as chronicled by AR. In this they were most ably supported by her cast of troupers playing AR's friends and acquaintances.

Gabriel Woolf read the part of the young AR. Through Gabriel's recordings of the S&A books, his voice has now become for many the voice of AR – and so it was tonight. The Japanese gentleman was played most inscrutably by Alan Hakim. He was almost impossible to recognise as our national treasurer beneath his excellent authentic costume, except his inscrutable demeanour gave him away. This was not unlike when he is asked to open the Society's coffers to pay out money.

Robert Thompson played the unpleasant actor most unpleasantly – a very difficult role as it required a complete contrast to his normal persona but the role did enable Robert to demonstrate his abundant musical talent performing Warlock's "Captain Stratton's Fancy", Ireland's "Sea Fever" to John Masefield's words, of course, Quilter's "Now Sleeps the Crimson Petal" and W.B. Yeats's song "The Salley Gardens". So, for that matter, did Flo Galbraith. She was excellent as the stately Scottish lady who brought her harp to the party – and was most definitely asked to play and sing.

The undoubted star of the evening was Jane Grell with her evocative retelling of the Annansee stories with full audience participation. Jane is a gifted storyteller (and incidentally not a

RANSOME CENTRE STAGE

Tar). AR describes that hearing Gypsy's stories "was to be carried back to the primitive days of story telling and to understand, a little, of how it was that the stories ... were handed on". We were privileged to witness something of this art at work in Durham this evening from Jane Grell – a far too brief example of the (almost lost) oral tradition.

We enjoyed a most delightful evening for which thanks are due to Kirsty and her troupe of players. Perhaps the occasion was "enhanced" by the ample provision of a wonderful libation 'opal hush', described by AR as a concoction of claret and lemonade. It is understood that the organising committee took their research into making 'opal hush' most seriously with lengthy tasting sessions to ensure it was as good as AR says it is.

Ransome described this night as his "first evening of friendliness in Chelsea". Whereas AR was to return to enjoy many more merry evenings at Gypsy's house, for the audience

BOHEMIA IN DURHAM

that night it was a once only experience, though one, it is suspected, long to be remembered, And after all did it matter that we were in Durham, not Chelsea? – not a jot. Remember AR's description: "Bohemia may be anywhere. It is a tint in the spectacles through which one sees the world in youth. It is not a place, but a state of mind." For a brief interlude we inhabited the state of mind that is Bohemia.

[In spite of what Malcolm says, it is reported that Robin Anderson declared Opal Hush to be "a waste of good claret".]

And here is the Japanese poet's part. As you will see, it lacks almost any context. I can only say, as the TARS Treasurer at the time, that whatever Malcolm says, I was never thinking of my Treasurer duties, but only of my embarrassing hat. It was in fact a priest's biretta, kindly lent by the Rev Brian Findlay, Kirsty's husband.

Japanese Poet: [*Your cue is "I owed a great deal to Yoshio Markino" – added by Young Ransome after "the quiet quizzical smile of the Japanese, who was making a sketch of the orator's face." It will come as the first interpolation, after about 2 minutes of Gabriel's reading (which includes some dialogue with Robert as the Actor).*]

In 1902, my Anglo-Japanese home at 151 Brixton Rd was an ordinary boarding-house occupied by an old couple and one step-daughter. I was then such an ambitious boy and I wanted 'name' – in vain. I used to write all that I felt in my note-book. It says: 'London is such a large town. It is really too large. Something like a big ship. I cannot move it with my strength. In London, if I try to make sound with London, London does not sound at all; only I hurt myself. That is all…'

One of those evenings my landlord came into my room and said 'A Japanese gentleman come to see you, sir.' The next second I met him on the middle of the stairs. It was my dear poet-friend, Yone Noguchi. Yone's four-month visit to London was my great comfort. We often had walk along the Victoria and Albert Embankment in nights to enjoy London fogs. I remember he made many poetries about London mists. I wonder if he ever published them. Yone thought the English publishers were too slow for the publication of his works, so he decided to publish them himself.

We saw the advertisements of those job-printers, and found out the one in Kennington was the fairest. Yone ordered him to print some two or three hundred copies of his few poetries on brown paper: it was about 16 pages, entitled 'From An Eastern Sea: by Yone Noguchi, a Japanese. Price: Two Shillings.' A messenger came from that printing office to see Yone especially about the lettering of the price. He asked Yone again and again to assure him it was really two shillings and not two pence! Yone gave him positive answer. After the messenger was gone, Yone told me that the messenger looked into his face so seriously to find out of Yone's head was 'a bit off'; and we laughed so much until our landlord's dog began to bark at us!

I think it was about the evening of Feb.13 1903, Yone and I went to the printing office, and a few hundred copies of 'From an Eastern Sea' was ready; so we carried them home. It was such a cold night and my hands had no feeling at all; then the pavement was quite frozen and it was almost impossible to walk with my worn-out boots. Yone warned me not to throw them on the mud because he could not afford to print them again!

Many people came to buy Yone's book. About business matter he was as bad as myself: he could not ask the payment. He presented each copy to everybody who came to buy. One evening he said to me: 'I cannot afford to present all my book.' I said: 'Of course you cannot; why don't you ask them the payment?' 'But, Markino, just think: how could I ask two shillings for this, although I put on that price?'

BOHEMIA IN DURHAM

When we were talking, a very young fellow came to buy Yone's book. It was Arthur Ransome: he was only 17 or 18 then. I told Ransome that Yone wanted two shillings a copy. Ransome was willing to pay. Yone shouted 'No, Markino, it is lie! It is lie!', and he ran out of the room. However, Ransome insisted to leave two shillings. We decided to buy some cigarettes, and when Ransome came we three should enjoy the smoking. Afterwards I learnt that Ransome was as poor as we were then.

Yone used to say that English peoples are so slow, and he would call me a cow because my temperament was so slow too. 'Markino,' he often exclaimed, 'you are getting too English altogether.' But one day he received a letter from his worshipped friend Mr Charles Warren Stoddart. It ran something like this: 'Yes, me dear Yone, you may think English people are very slow; you may not like them now. But be patient and stay there a little longer. Some day you will find out something at the bottom of English people's hearts – some gentleness, some sweetness, what other nations seldom have. When you have once recognised this, you will not forget it all your life.'

Yone was a very sharp observer. It did not take him long to fall in love with the English peoples. Indeed, after only four months' stay in London, when I went to see him off at Paddington Station, I saw his eyes were much inflammated with tears. He peeped out of the train window and said to me: 'I am sure I shall come back to England. Yes, I must come back again. I promise you faithfully. So you wait here until I come.' But he had gone so soon.

RANSOME CENTRE STAGE

Gabriel Woolf (AR), Kirsty Nichol Findlay (producer), Alan Hakim (Japanese Poet)

Our last two contributions are not strictly entitled to appearance in an anthology of TARS performances, but are so relevant that we are including them.

First, a play that was to be produced in Otley, but had to be called off – after being publicised and tickets sold for the Christmas season of 2012. Duncan Hall, one of its originators, will explain.

Introduction
by
Duncan Hall

My brother, Nick, and I worked together to dramatise *Winter Holiday* for the stage. I had previously written part of a radio play script for it that had received some interest from the BBC but then went nowhere as these things often do.

We are both Ransome "super-fans", both had lots of writing experience (e.g. my *Brambleholme* series of children's books) and Nick had worked in theatre groups in various capacities, including as a director, and also as a tour manager (and later cast member) for a popular production of *The Life of Pi*.

We had gone to the West Yorkshire Playhouse together to see a big Christmas production of *The Secret Garden* and immediately got to talking about the idea of a stage play of *Winter Holiday* being the ideal winter family production. It seemed so obvious, it was almost a surprise that nobody had done it before (as far as I know!)

We had also seen a weird and wonderful clown performance at the Alhambra theatre in Bradford (where Nick worked at the time) called *Slava's Snow Show* which had some really inventive ideas about creating on-stage snow and weather, and the performance "ended" with a big "snowball" fight, including the audience. We liked the idea of incorporating some of those ideas into our *Winter Holiday* play.

The original idea was to include original songs too. Nick and I are a song-writing/performing duo (The Hall Brothers), we already had a couple of songs that would fit and would write more. It wasn't intended to be a musical, as such, but a play with a few songs.

We set about writing the first draft of the script in earnest and then approached the Ransome literary estate about it and quickly got a positive response. I had had previous dealings with the executors about trying to get permission to call a song *Swallows and Amazons* and ideas about a Ransome bird book and a children's picture book of *Swallows and Amazons* in verse (that one did get the green light from the executors and other copyright holders, but failed to find an enthusiastic publisher.)

The issue was then about who would perform it and where. Nick had worked previously with an impressive amateur group in Otley – the Otley Community Players – and we decided that they would be a good way to get the play performed and on stage. Nick was the director; a cast came together quickly, rehearsals were pretty good... We had adults playing the children – like the *Swallows and Amazons* stage play – and some great people involved. The amateur cast included some good singers and musicians.

A range of factors conspired to make it clear that it wasn't going to be ready for the original planned date of performance. This was a shame – there'd been articles in the local newspapers, posters around town, tickets sold. The local theatre where it was going to be put on found us a new date, a couple of months later, but unfortunately several key cast members couldn't make the new date. It was postponed and finally shelved.

The script has been "gathering dust" on a laptop hard drive ever since. With hindsight, it was probably too ambitious a project for an amateur group – however ambitious and talented – because it just needed more time and resources than we had to get it realised on stage in the way that we had pictured it when we wrote it. I'd still love to see it on a stage…

WINTER HOLIDAY

SCENE 1 – FARM, MORNING

Scene opens with Dick lying in bed in his room halfway up the scaff. tower upstage right. Dorothea runs up the stairs excitedly and shakes him.

Dorothea: Dick! Are you awake?

Dick: Well I am now.

Dorothea: It's snowed!

Dick sits up, much more alert, and puts on his glasses.

Dick: What?

Dorothea: It's snowed overnight! It must have been blizzarding! Look!

They both go over to the 'window' and look out.

Dick: Gosh! The farm looks so different!

Enter Mrs Dixon up the stairs from below.

Mrs Dixon: Seven and eight and nine and ten and eleven and twelve and that's the dozen!

Dick: It's snowed Mrs Dixon!

Mrs Dixon: Good morning Dick! Good morning Dorothea! Aye it's snowed right enough. It's been that cold these past weeks it's a miracle it's not snowed like this before. There's ice in the jugs this morning so I've brought you some hot water. No need to start the day freezing.

Dorothea: Thank you!

Mrs Dixon: Right, come on! Breakfast!

Mrs Dixon leads the way and Dick and Dot follow. Down below on the stage Mr Dixon has entered, carrying in a table and placing in between the open 'windows' upstage centre. Dick and Dot pull up a chair each and sit down

Dick: There are 12 steps, she's quite right!

Mrs Dixon: Right! Porridge, then bacon!

The children look at each other, unused to such brisk ways

Mrs Dixon: Tuck in! I'm not going to make visitors of you!

Dick & Dot look at each other, then tuck in.

Dick & Dot: (*between mouthfuls*) Morning Mr Dixon!

Mr Dixon looks at them shyly and starts to exit.

Mr Dixon: Good morning to you.

He exits. Mrs Dixon laughs at Dick & Dot's slightly crestfallen faces.

Mrs Dixon: Eee, he's not one for talking isn't Dixon! Well what have you got planned for your first day?

Dick: Well first I need to find a good place for an observatory.

OTLEY – WINTER HOLIDAY

Mrs Dixon: Eh?

Dick: An observatory. For looking at stars.

Mrs Dixon: Oh right!

Dorothea: And there are a million other things we want to look at as well!

Mrs Dixon: (laughs) Eee, that's your mother all over! Well, you look all you want, but dinner will be ready at half past twelve and you'd best be here if you want any.

Dorothea: Come on Dick, let's get going!

Music plays as Mrs Dixon takes the table off and exits as Dick and Dot remove the chairs and quickly put coats, gloves, hats, scarves and wellies over their pyjamas. They close the 'windows' which become the outside of the farm house. They step forward, wrap their arms around themselves, blow on their hands and look around to indicate being outside. Mr Dixon and Old Silas enter, Old Silas is pushing a wheelbarrow of firewood

Dick & Dot: Hello Silas! Hello Mr Dixon!

Mr Dixon: Hello.

He exits quickly, leaving Old Silas shaking his head and chuckling.

Old Silas: Ee! He's not one for talking isn't Dixon! Nah then! Brought your skates with you?

Dick: Yes! Has the lake frozen then?

Old Silas: (*chuckles*) Nay, it'll be a while before the lake freezes. It's not often it does. But it's been a grand year for hollyberry and that's a sign.

Dorothea: Is there anywhere else we could skate?

Old Silas: Aye. Yon tarn up by the old barn. You'll be skating on there if we have another night like last. Any road. Things to do...

He starts to trundle offstage with his barrow.

Dorothea: Thank you!

Exit Old Silas.

Dick: Let's go up to the tarn.

Dorothea: No. let's go to the lake first!

SCENE 2 – LAKE, MORNING

They move round the stage to music as the windows are covered in a white cloth. They sit on half an upturned boat (which will double as another prop on the other side), far stage left, clearing snow off it first.

Dick: A boat! They must have put it like this for the winter, to keep rain and snow out of it. Look at that island!

Dick gets his telescope out. They look up and out to the balcony.

Dorothea: What a pity. I wish we could row. "They launched their trusty vessel, put out their oars and rowed out to the mysterious island across the deserted lake, where no-one had ever rowed before...!"

OTLEY – WINTER HOLIDAY

Dick: There's somebody rowing now!

Dorothea: Give me the telescope!

Dick hands her the telescope. She puts it to her eye.

Dorothea: "the marooned sailors rowed desperately, taking their wounded friend to the safety of the island…"

Dick: Oh give it here!

Dot reluctantly hands the telescope back

Dorothea: I can see just as well without it anyway.

Dick puts it to his eye.

Dick: Hullo! Dot! They're not grown-up!

The Swallows and Amazons are up on the balcony behind the lighting desk

Susan: Put your coat on Roger!

Roger: Aye, aye sir!

Titty: Let's go to the old harbour!

Nancy: Give way oars!

Dick: They're on the island. Lucky things. I do wish this boat was in the water.

Dorothea: Even if it was we can't row.

Dick: It looks easy.

Dorothea: It's no good even thinking about it.

Dick: What are they doing now?

The Swallows and the Amazons start flapping flags quickly at each other – Susan, John and Nancy on the right of the balcony and Titty, Roger and Peggy at the left.

Dorothea: Signalling! Is it for us?

Dick: No. They're flapping at each other. Looks like they're practising.

Nancy: Peggy you donkey! That's all wrong! Try it again!

Dick: Looks like great fun! *Pause.*

Dorothea: It's awfully cold standing about like this.

Dick: What's up?

Dorothea: "The Outcasts, by Dorothea Callum. The two children, brother and sister, shared their last few crumbs and looked up and down the deserted shore. Was this the end?" *Pause.*

Dick: Shall we go and find an observatory?

Dorothea: Yes. Bother them!

SCENE 3 – OBSERVATORY, MORNING

Dick and Dorothea walk around the stage to music. They approach the scaff. tower

Dick: Look at that barn. It's the very place for an observatory.

Dorothea: The very place for a story. And look at the lake!

They look out across the auditorium

Dick: Dot, I bet that's the farmhouse where those children are staying.

OTLEY – WINTER HOLIDAY

Dorothea: Bother them. How about your observatory? Won't it be rather cold here at night?

Dick: Rather. (*He walks into the barn, near the bottom of the steps*).

Dick starts to climb the stairs

Dorothea: Careful Dick!

Dick: It feels very solid. Come on.

Dorothea gingerly follows up the steps

Dick: What a place to look out from. We'll be able to see all the northern stars.

Dorothea tries to look enthusiastic

Dick: You can see that farmhouse better from here.

Dorothea: We might not like them even if we met them.

Dick: Let's find some wood for this evening and see if the ice is bearing on the tarn. Then we had better get down for Mrs. Dixon's tea. Oh look! There's that boat.

He reaches for his telescope and starts looking out across the auditorium again.

Dorothea: Where?

Dick: There. Turning into the bay by the farmhouse. I said that was where they were from.

Dick: They're from that farmhouse. The boat has gone away again just with the two redcaps, but I can see the other children by the house.

Dorothea: Come on Dick. What's the good of thinking about them? They might as well be in some different world.

Dick: Why not?! Why not? Just wait till dark and we can try signalling to Mars!

Dorothea: To Mars?

Dick: Why not? Of course they may not see it. And even if they do they may not understand it. A different world, you see. It makes it even more like signalling to Mars.

Dorothea: That's a great idea. Come on, we'll be late for tea.

Blackout then lights up – dim and blue

SCENE 4 – OBSERVATORY, EVENING

Music. Dick and Dot switch on torches.

Dorothea: I thought supper would never end.

Dick: There's Cassiopeia. It's supposed to look like her chair. But none of them look anything like what they're supposed to. Even the plough looks more like a cart...

Dorothea: When will we start?

Dick: Start what?

Dorothea: Signalling to Mars!

Dick: Oh them. Not yet. No point till they're going to bed or they won't see. It's too early yet. Why not light a fire?

Dorothea: Bother. I forgot to bring newspaper and

matches.

Dick: Never mind.

Dick: Can you use the torch to see what the book says? Get the chapter on the January sky.

Dorothea: Got it.

Dick: I've got the plough. And the Pole Star. What else should I look out for?

Dorothea: Taurus. The Bull.

Dick: Oh bother the bull. It won't look anything like one. I've got the Pleiades! Come and look.

Dick offers her the telescope.

Dorothea: I can see a lot better without.

Dick: How many of the Pleiades can you see?

Dorothea: (*counts in her head*) Six?

Dick: There are lots more than that. But it's awfully hard to see them when the telescope moves around so much.

A small light shines out from the balcony

Dorothea: Look, look. Dick. I think a light has gone on upstairs!

Dick: What? You made me jump.

Dorothea: Well you should hang out a sign when you're not in. There's a light on Mars.

Dick looks through the telescope

Dick: Let's begin signalling at once. They must have just gone upstairs.

Dorothea: Will they be looking out?

Dick: They might. They might be looking for a signal from Earth! Let's try with the torch.

Dick takes the torch and hides it behind his hand. He takes it out again and does the same repeatedly, producing three long flashes.

Dorothea: Nothing

Dick: Use the telescope. The Martians may reply any minute.

Dick produces the three long flashes again.

Dorothea: (*Looking through telescope*) Perhaps it isn't their room. Perhaps that light has nothing to do with them. It's the farm woman who has gone to see how much mud and snow they brought in with them, because they came in without using the doormat. She's down on her hands and knees and scrubbing, and very cross indeed. And naturally she isn't looking this way…

Dick: Dot, you can't see all that through the telescope?

Dorothea: Of course I can't. I can never see anything through the telescope!

Dick: I might as well try again. It may be two or three nights before they see us.

Dick produces the three long flashes again.

Pause

Dorothea: It's awfully cold. And we must get back to Mrs. Dixon's.

Dick: One more time. (*The light at the back of the theatre goes out*) Hullo. Has the light gone off?

Dorothea: Yes. Perhaps it was them after all, and they've gone to bed.

It comes back on again

Dick: It's back. Something's happening…

Off again. On again.

Dick: If it happens again…

Off again

Dick: They've answered.

Dorothea: What are we going to do?

Dick: Give them the signal again. That'll settle it

The light at the back of the auditorium starts going on and off in a series of dots and dashes

Dorothea: They're trying to say something…

Dick: (*Sadly*) Morse code. And we don't know it.

Dorothea: Morse… Martian…

Dick: True… Naturally we don't know their language. We'll make our first signal again to show we don't understand.

Dick makes the three flashes again and it is echoed from the back of the theatre

Dick: We can't do any more tonight.

Dorothea: They'll come to see what it was in the morning. We simply must be here first.

Blackout, music

SCENE 5 – OBSERVATORY/TARN, MORNING MEETING

Lights up – Morning – Dick and Dot are at the foot of the tower.

Dorothea: They may be here any second.

Dick pulls out his telescope

Dick: Hullo! I can see them! There, not far away.

Dorothea: Where?

Dick: You'll see them in a second.

Dorothea: Oh yes, here they come. Are they going to come straight across that stream?

Dick: They can't. The ice isn't bearing yet. At least, it wasn't yesterday.

There is a loud splash from the back of the auditorium and some shocked laughter.

Dorothea: Oh no! Now they'll have to turn back and change their shoes…

Dick: No, they're still coming.

John, Susan, Titty, Roger, Nancy and Peggy enter from the back of the auditorium, round the seating on the right hand side, entering stage left.

Dorothea: Come on. We signalled to them, so we had better go and meet them.

Dick: All right but… but you do the talking.

They come down the stairs and walk towards the front of the stage. The Swallows and Amazons pace grimly on. Titty waves a white handkerchief on a stick

Dorothea: The flag is to show it's peace. Can you tie my handkerchief onto your telescope?

Dick: Just wave it.

Dorothea pulls out her handkerchief and waves it. The Swallows and Amazons continue forwards and enter the stage.

Dick looks across at Dorothea to say something. Dorothea looks back.

Titty: I don't believe they're in distress at all!

Roger: (*very disappointed*) Don't they want to be rescued from anything?

Dick: We were just signalling to Mars.

John: To Mars?

Titty: Not to us?

Dorothea: We wanted you to answer. It was Dick's idea to be signalling to Mars. You see, we didn't know you…

Nancy: Jib-booms and Bobstays, what a good idea!

Dick: And of course, when you started answering in Martian, we couldn't understand.

John: Morse code. We asked what was the matter, and then I took a bearing with the compass.

Dorothea: We saw you on the lake yesterday.

Roger: We saw you too.

Nancy: (*impatiently*) Well we're all here now anyway. Right, what are you?

Dorothea: Well... (*uncertainly*) our name is Callum. He's Dick, and I'm Dorothea.

Nancy: Yes, yes, Dick and Dorothea, but *what* are you? We're explorers and sailors!

Dorothea: Dick's an astronomer.

Dick: And Dorothea writes stories.

Nancy: Right. I'm Nancy Blackett. Captain of the *Amazon*. This is Peggy, mate of the *Amazon*. This is Captain John Walker, of the *Swallow*, Susan, mate of the *Swallow*, Titty is their able-seaman and Roger is their ship's boy.

Dick: Was that the *Amazon*? The boat we saw you in yesterday?

Nancy: (*horrified*) That? That was a rowing boat! *Amazon* is out of the water for the winter. We use the rowing boat every day to come over to Holly Howe, or to Rio. That's our name for the village. (*To Dick*) An astronomer? I expect you've come to the Arctic to see the eclipse.

Dick: But there isn't going to be an eclipse.

Nancy: No? Well, Holly Howe Farm isn't Mars! Don't be so particular!

Dick: (*laughing*) Why the Arctic?

Nancy: (*to the other Swallows and Amazons*) Should we tell them? That Mars idea was jolly good.

Titty: Tell them.

A pause. Nancy then squats down and the others follow

suit.

Nancy: Well you know what it's like. Dark at tea-time and sleeping indoors: nothing ever happens in the winter holidays. We had to think of something we could do while our ships were out of the water. And something where it would be all right for us to be sleeping in beds rather than tents… So we started a Polar Expedition. We sleep in the Eskimo settlements at night, same as you, and we've been building an igloo as a base.

Peggy: The idea was that as soon as we could, we would go to the North Pole over the ice… we've got a brilliant North Pole…

Nancy: (*jumping up and gesturing out towards the audience*) But the beastly Arctic won't freeze. And there's only one week of holiday left. The snow will help, but it just isn't freezing fast enough. The lake's just too deep.

John: Let's have a look at your Signal Station.

Dick: Observatory.

They all walk towards the barn

Nancy: Ouch, my feet are frozen. How are yours Peggy?

Peggy: Icicles.

Nancy: We were galoots going through the ice…

Dorothea: Shall I light the fire? We've brought up some newspaper this morning…

Susan: Newspaper? For lighting a fire?

Nancy: We'd better show you how to light a fire with no paper and only one match… I say, we'd better get home

and warm-up! I say, let's all meet at the tarn in the morning and go skating!
All: Hurrah!

SCENE 6 – SKATING ON THE TARN

All the children are sitting by the side of the tarn – Nancy, John, Susan and Peggy, stage right. Roger, Titty and Dick stage left.. Dot enters stage right, carrying a pair of skates – She is unseen as she overhears the following conversation..

Nancy: What a lovely day for skating! (*conspiratorially*) I say you three – what do we think of the Ds?
John: That signalling to Mars was a good idea.
Peggy: Yes, but fancy having an idea like that and then not knowing any Morse code!
Nancy: An astronomer could be quite useful...
Peggy: But what's she going to do?
Dorothea looks uncomfortable and tiptoes quickly over to sit next to Dick.
John: It would be pretty beastly to leave them out of things now.
Nancy: True. Come on! Shake a leg, me hearties. Get those skates on.
They all fumble with the straps of their skates. Dick sets off

OTLEY – WINTER HOLIDAY

skating across the tarn

Titty: But he can skate…

Roger: Like anything!

Dick twirls around and starts to skate back

Nancy: Why didn't you tell us? Of course you should be in the polar expedition. Not one of us can skate like that!

Dick: (*returning across the tarn and reaching out his hands*) Come on Dot, this is lots better than doing it indoors.

Nancy: Can you skate too?

Dorothea reaches out to Dick and they skate off together with linked arms, skating in time with each other

Dorothea: They're letting us be part of it. Because of your skating. Nancy just said so.

Dick: Part of what?

Nancy skates out to meet them, less gracefully.

Nancy: Hey, you teach me how to twiddle around and go backwards and what not, and I'll teach you signalling.

Dick: You just put your weight on one foot and swing yourself around. (*Dick does this*) That's what it feels like anyway.

Nancy: Like this? (*swings around dramatically and falls heavily onto the ice*). Not quite like that… (*She climbs up*) Show me slowly…

They continue practising in the background. Susan and John skate out very slowly and carefully. Peggy skates sturdily like Nancy. Roger keeps trying to skate like Dick and keeps falling over. Titty moves VERY slowly, inch by inch.

Dorothea: (*To Titty*) Can I help?

Titty: No, no. I'm going to do it by myself...

Music (and song?) for skating – sort of a dance routine based around the various people's skating prowess or otherwise! Everybody collapses exhausted on the shore of the tarn.

Nancy: Come on then Dick. I need to show you Morse code.

Dick: Please. I've got my pocket book.

They walk up to the barn. The others carry on skating

Nancy: So these are the letters with the dots and dashes. So you can do that with short and long flashes, when you're signalling to Holly Howe from up here. It can be done with flags as well.

Dick: Was that what you were doing on the island, yesterday?

Nancy: No – that was semaphore. I'll write you the alphabet down for that as well. You should learn them both. And John's had an idea for another way of signalling between here and Holly Howe. They'll be ready by tomorrow.

Dick: Should we just go straight to Holly Howe tomorrow?

Nancy: Come up here first, so we can try out these new signals. And then Mother has invited you and Dorothea to join us all for lunch tomorrow at our house!

Dick: How kind! Where is your house?

Nancy: Beckfoot. Look out there, across the wide Arctic

OTLEY – WINTER HOLIDAY

Sea. Can you see there's a kind of high promontory? Past all the islands? With a wood behind? The promontory's all heather and rock.

Dick gets his telescope and looks

Dick: With a flagstaff on the end?

Nancy: That's the one.

Dick: Could we signal to you from here?

Nancy: It's too far, really. Although you could see a flag on the staff from here, couldn't you? I know – I'll run a big flag up there when we mean to start for the North Pole. They can see it from just above Holly Howe, and you can see it from here.

Dick: Hang on, I'll just write that down. Flag…at…Beckfoot… Start…for…Pole.

Nancy: I just hope it keeps freezing. We might be able to skate part of the way…

Dick: Does the whole lake freeze?

Nancy: It has done. Not since we were born, but Mother remembers it. And everybody says it's going to happen this year. But it really is taking its time over it. It will be a terrible waste for it to be frozen end to end while we're all at school. Hullo, are they signalling?

Roger is doing Semaphore signals. Dick is trying to follow from what's written in his pocketbook, but Nancy says the letters as they come…

Nancy: L…A…Z…Y…B…O…N…E…S Lazybones? Shiver my timbers! The cheek! Come on, let's have one more skate before heading home.

SCENE 7 – ARCTIC VOYAGE

Next morning at the barn (signals - diamond over north cone – are hung on the balcony). Dick and Dot are at the foot of the scaff tower. John enters, carrying whitewashed signals

John: Morning. Right, I've put some signals up on the side of the house. How do they look?

Dick and Dorothea look across and see the signals (at Holly Howe)

Dorothea: Oh they're as clear as anything.

Dick: But what do they mean?

John: Whatever we like. We need to draw up a key. We thought that one could be "Come to Holly Howe" but we'll want them for "Come to the Igloo" or "Come to the tarn". Anyway, I need to rig this up and see how they react at Holly Howe.

John reaches as high as he can and mimes hammering in a nail. He hangs the signals on a string to the side of the barn

John: Watch what happens…

Dick puts his telescope up to his eye. On the balcony Susan changes the signal.

Dick: They're taking it down

John: Good. That means they could see it. Great stuff. They're in a rush. Nancy and Peggy must be in sight. Come on, let's get down to the lake.

They dash down to the shore of the lake – a jetty near Holly Howe. Susan, Titty and Roger enter.

OTLEY – WINTER HOLIDAY

Roger: Morning! There's quite a lot of ice in the bay. The postman told Mrs Jackson that there'll be skating in the bay by the town by tonight.

Titty: Oh if only it would hurry up and freeze the whole lake…

Susan: Peggy's nearly here, but she's going to struggle to bring the boat in.

John: Just Peggy? That's odd. Oh here she comes.

Titty: She's met an iceberg!

Roger: She's going to ram it! (*Smash of ice*)

Susan: Looks like she's coming for the jetty, ice or no ice… (*More smashing*)

Titty: Don't fall in!

Peggy: (*From offstage*) Teach your grandmother!

Peggy arrives at side of stage which has become a jetty, carrying the end of a length of rope.

Peggy: (*grinning*) Nancy will be jolly sorry she missed that!

John: Where is Nancy?

Peggy: Oh she's got a bit of jaw ache. All aboard! Are you two accustomed to boats?

Dick and Dorothea: No…

Peggy: Well just do what Susan does and sit down as soon as you're on board. It's horribly easy to tip her over when we're all clambering about.

Roger: And a cold bath if you do!

Exit by seating stage left – music covers picture of Beckfoot coming up on the screen – actors move round seating and arrive stage right.

SCENE 8 – BECKFOOT, DOCTOR AND MUMPS

Peggy: Right, we're here. Home sweet home! Hullo, where's Nancy?

Dorothea: Something's wrong.

John: She's probably lurking somewhere...

Peggy: Probably still toasting her jaw. She did say it was very stiff. Come on anyway.

Mrs Blackett enters.

Mrs Blackett: (*worried/distracted*) Oh Peggy, I do wish you had waited... Now, you mustn't think I'm not very pleased to see you all, but I'm not at all sure I should let you in the house.

Peggy: But Mother! You invited them!

Mrs Blackett: What is it poor Nancy calls you? Galoot isn't it? Of course I invited them! Can you go along to the road and try to catch the doctor? I've telephoned but he's been up the valley to tend to a broken ankle. Don't come in the house.

Peggy: Is it Nancy?

Mrs Blackett: Of course it's Nancy. Now go along and

hold up the doctor. Ask him to come and have a look at her. (*realises that Dick and Dot are startled*) Oh I'm so sorry – Dick and Dorothea isn't it? Good to meet you and sorry about all this!

She waves in a friendly manner and exits left as the children move round the stage to stand centre

Susan: I wonder if Nancy is really ill?

Peggy: She never is. Anyway, she must have been very quick about it. It was only a jaw ache when I left.

Dorothea: Mrs Blackett thinks she is.

Peggy: Oh that's just mother. Anyway, we'll give the doctor a bit of a shock.

Dorothea: He's probably accustomed to illness.

Peggy: Holding him up I mean!

John: It will be awful if Nancy is too ill to come to the Pole.

Peggy: Of course she'll be all right. She planned the whole thing and she isn't going to miss it now.

Titty: What if the doctor's gone already?

Dick: (*crouching down and looking at the snow*) He hasn't.

Dorothea: How do you know?

Dick: A car has been that way, with snow chains on. It hasn't come back again yet.

John crouches down next to Dick.

John: Not half bad.

Peggy: Right, we'll spread ourselves out along the road.

By the time he's passed seven of us all jumping up and down and shouting like fury, he'll know that something's up.

Dick: Listen!

John: He's coming.

We hear a car approaching in the distance. They spread themselves out.

Peggy: Aaaarggggh!!

John: Stop!!

Dick: Stop, stop!

Roger shrieks. The doctor enters at speed, holding an old-fashioned steering wheel.

Doctor: Hullo!!!

The car stops. Dorothea runs to join it, Susan and Roger, the others all enter and gather around the 'car'.

Doctor: What on earth?!

Peggy: Nancy's got toothache. Mother asked us to stop you and see if you can come and see her...

Doctor: Toothache? How many of you are there? I know Peggy...

Peggy: These are the Swallows...

Doctor: Ah, the famous Swallows. And these two?

Peggy: Dick and Dorothea.

Doctor: Well the car's built for four, so we should be able to manage a mere eight. All jump aboard. I can only have one in the front with me. Hop in... Dorothy did they say your name was?

Dorothea: Dorothea. Or Dot.

Doctor: Come on the rest of you. The extra weight will probably help. Make sure the door's shut.

They pretend to cram into the 'car' and they set off, jiggling about.

Doctor: Everybody's saying the whole lake is going to freeze if it keeps on like this.

Peggy: What's the good? We've only three days more left of the holiday?

Doctor: Ah, I'd forgotten that. Here we are.

He pulls up outside Beckfoot.
Mrs Blackett enters, opening the 'windows' to show that they are now inside the house.

Mrs Blackett: Will you come straight up Doctor? I'm so glad they were able to catch you. The children can wait in the study for a few minutes… Not in the dining room, Peggy. Nancy was in there a long time…

They all look at each other worriedly as the Doctor and Mrs Blackett exit left

Peggy: This is Uncle Jim's study.

Titty: We call him Captain Flint

Peggy: He uses it when he's not abroad and not on the houseboat.

Dick: What houseboat?

Peggy: It's on the lake. Between Holly Howe and the island. He's abroad at the moment or we would have visited.

RANSOME CENTRE STAGE

The Doctor and Mrs Blackett enter from scaffold

Doctor: Mumps, my dear madam, mumps. She'll have a face like a pumpkin tomorrow.

Mrs Blackett: Should she stay in bed?

Doctor: Yes, yes. Stay in bed and keep warm. The quicker the swelling comes, the quicker it will go down. Probably three or four weeks...

Mrs Blackett: Three or four weeks until she can go back to school?

Doctor: No, she'll be infectious for at least another week after the swelling has gone down...

They continue to walk through the house, so that they have exited before the end of the next exchange.

Mrs Blackett: What about Peggy?

Doctor: You will have to isolate her, of course. Not that it really matters... Some schools...

Exit Doctor and Mrs Blackett right.

Susan: If it's mumps, she won't be able to go to the North Pole.

John: Well, we can't go then.

Peggy: We'll have to put it off for another year.

Titty: We might not be here another year. Not in winter...

Nancy, enters from "upstairs" left and does a poor owl call. The others hear and gather round her.

Nancy: (*whispering*) Mumps

Susan: We know. We're so sorry.

OTLEY – WINTER HOLIDAY

John: There's no point in going to the Pole without you. It wouldn't be fair anyway.

Nancy laughs but then it hurts so she stops.

Nancy: Galoots! Donks! Idiots! Turnipheads! It's the very best thing that could have happened. Don't you see? It's saved everything! It's added a whole month to the holidays. The Lake will be frozen from end to end long before a month is up…

Peggy: It won't be much of an expedition with just one?

Roger: We'll all be at school.

Nancy: Will you?! Will you?!? Galoots the lot of you! That was the first thing I asked him!

Enter Mrs Blackett and Doctor right.

Mrs Blackett: Nancy!! Go back to bed this minute!

Nancy: Ask him yourself. (*exits*)

Doctor: She means we can't get rid of you. They won't let you back at school until I say that there's no chance of you getting mumps, or giving it to everybody else when you get there.

Roger starts thinking through the implications of this

Mrs Blackett: There's a spare room at Mrs Jackson's, isn't there Susan?

Susan: Yes.

Mrs Blackett: Right. Well we'll have to ask her to put Peggy in it. The doctor very kindly says he'll drive you round, so Peggy will go with you now. Now then, you Swallows. Your mother told me she was leaving the health papers with one of you for me to sign before you go back.

John: I've got them.

Mrs Blackett: If they're the same as Nancy and Peggy's then you won't be able to go back either. I don't know what your mother will say.

Roger: Not... not go back to school?

Doctor: No.

Titty: For how long?

Doctor: About a month, I suppose. Unless one of you gets mumps too, and then it'll be longer still. None of you feels like it now, I suppose? Any stiff jaws?

They all intimate that they are fine.

Mrs Blackett: (*To Dorothea*) And what about you two? Have you got certificates to sign too?

Dorothea: Mother put them in an envelope and gave them to Mrs Dixon.

Mrs Blackett: Well I'm coming round to see Mrs Jackson this afternoon about Peggy. I might as well carry on and see Mrs Dixon too. Off you go now, you mustn't keep the doctor waiting. (*To the Doctor*) I suppose it's all right my going round there this afternoon, after being with Nancy.

Doctor: Don't kiss her. Or Peggy either.

Mrs Blackett: I don't want to. Horrid little wretches both of them (*pulls a face at Peggy to show she is just joking*)

Roger: What about lunch?

Mrs Blackett: You'll just have to have it at Holly Howe.

Doctor: In you go. Room for everybody. We ride... to Holly

Howe!

They climb back in the car and drive off, jiggling about. They 'arrive' at Holly Howe farm. Dick, Dorothea, Nancy, Peggy, Susan, Roger, Titty, the Doctor, Mrs Jackson all present.

SCENE 9 – HOLLY HOWE AND HOLIDAY FORMS

John: Hullo Mrs Jackson! (*he exits left to get medical papers*)

Mrs Jackson: Ee, here you are! Your mother's just telephoned me Miss Peggy. So Miss Nancy's got mumps. And Peggy's to sleep here. And none of you have had a bite to eat. Ee, it's a good thing I've got yon cold roast beef to cut at.

Doctor: Nobody's ever gone hungry at your house yet, Mrs Jackson.

John enters with certificates as Mrs Jackson exits. The Doctor looks at them briefly.

Doctor: Yes, they're the same. Well good luck to you all. I'll be around every now and then to check in on you. Make sure you let me know the moment anybody's jaw starts to feel stiff.

Exit Doctor. Susan takes one of the certificates from John and shows it to Dorothea.

Susan: There. There's no getting out of it. The things can't be signed.

Peggy: Who wants to get out of it? Nancy said herself that it's the very best thing that could have happened.

Titty: It's really like the Christmas holiday was just starting now.

Roger: Of course it's too late now, or we could have put an advertisement in the newspaper.

Susan: What?

Roger: Mumps for anyone who wants them. Anybody'd be willing to pay quite a lot of their pocket money for an extra month of holiday!

All laugh

Roger: Why not? Nancy could charge sixpence just to shake hands with people. But it's too late now.

Peggy: Why too late?

Roger: By the time the advert was in, they'd all be back at school.

John: Money-grubbing brute.

Roger: Well... she could shake hands for free with people she really liked!

Susan: (*To Dorothea*) Are your papers the same?

Dorothea: I don't know. Perhaps not all schools are alike.

John: I bet they are. No school wants people with faces like pumpkins, or whatever. I'm sure they all do their best to keep clear of any type of plague...

Titty: Plague... Of course Roger's wrong. Everybody will want to keep away from us. If it was summer we'd hoist a yellow flag on Swallow…

Dick: Why yellow?

John: Quarantine. To show that we've come from a plague port. And Nancy would need a plague flag. Yellow and black squares.

Titty: Let's make her one!

Susan: Good idea. I'm sure Mrs Jackson has some spare bits of cloth.

Titty: We'll need one to hoist from the North Pole when we get there.

Mrs Blackett enters

Mrs Blackett: Right, I've been to visit Mrs Dixon. Oh, she can talk! I heard about Silas' rheumatism, about pork pies, elderberry wine and pretty much every other subject. But I'm afraid your certificates are quite the same as the others. Mrs Dixon's stuck with you I'm afraid.

Peggy: Three million cheers.

Mrs Blackett: That is hardly appropriate. Oh and by the way, I've got a message for you all from Nancy.

Peggy: (*reads*) "Make Wildcat Spitzbergen… Try Alaska… Cross Greenland."

Dorothea: I don't understand!

Peggy: We can't do Spitzbergen yet. Not until we can get to Wild Cat Island by ice.

Titty: What about Alaska?

Peggy: Greenland's better. I know where she means. It's the country up on the fells above the tarn. A real wilderness. Jib-booms and bobstays! We shall cross Greenland tomorrow.

Roger: It will be quite a crossing. Seven dogs on the sled...

Mrs Blackett: Just you be careful – I don't want any more invalids!

Music covers as they all exit.

SCENE 10 – CROSSING GREENLAND, CRAGFAST SHEEP

Enter John, Susan and Peggy stage left, trudging through the snow. They end up far stage right.

John: How are those dogs doing?

Susan: Oh they're miles behind!

Peggy: We'd better take the sledge again.

Enter Titty, Dick, Dot and Roger stage left pulling a laden sledge slowly on ropes. They look shattered.

Titty: I knew crossing Greenland was going to be hard work, but this is ridiculous!

Dot: The mountains look so beautiful covered in snow! I wish I knew all their names like Peggy does.

Titty: (*stops and throws down the rope*) That's it! It's hotter than it is in summer!

Susan: (*calls*) It won't be if you don't keep moving!

Roger: Well, we're jolly hot now!

A strange mewing sound is heard (played on the violin). Dick looks up towards the balcony and shades his eyes.

Dick: Is it those two big birds making that noise?

Peggy: Buzzards. They're calling to each other. You often see them up on the crags.

Dick: I've seen them in books.

John, Susan and Peggy take the ropes from the younger ones.

Roger: Good strong dogs!

John: Watch it!

Roger: Let's take the alpine rope in case of accidents and go on ahead. The dogs are sure to follow.

Peggy: Shiver my timbers! Sure to follow indeed! Come on!

John, Peggy and Susan dash off stage right with the sledge.

Titty: Don't go so fast!

Roger: I wish we had ice axes too.

Titty: Hi Dick, you've got to make a loop for yourself in the rope.

Dick: (*follows the buzzards with his gaze as they fly over to the scaff. tower*) Do you think they've got a nest up there?

Roger: Who?

Dick: The buzzards! Shall we go and have a look?

Roger: Yes come on! It's our turn to explore! Good job we got the rope!

Titty: Yes, we can't exactly get lost. Let's go up there on the ridge and see where the dogs have got to.

They climb up to the highest point of the scaff. tower, covered by music.

Roger: There they are! They're miles away already! Good dogs! Good dogs!

Titty: We ought to go after them. They don't know we've gone a different way.

Dick: There's something down there on the ledge. It could be a nest.

Dot: I think we ought to go back. They're a tremendous way ahead.

Dick: (*looking through the telescope*) It's not a nest. It's a sheep. A dead sheep.

Roger: Let's have a look!

Dot: But it's not dead.

Halfway up the scaff. tower a puppeteer in black makes the crag fast sheep's head move and makes a bleating sound.

Dot: Poor thing. It's probably starving.

Titty: That does happen to sheep on fells. Especially when there's a bit of snow.

Roger: How are we going to get it down?

Dick: I'll climb down to the ledge with the rope. You'll have to hold onto the other end up here. Then I'll tie it round the sheep and you'll be able to lower it down. It'll be perfectly safe.

Titty: But what will you do on the ledge without a rope

while we're lowering it down?

Dick: I'll just sit on the ledge. It'll just be like sitting on a chair. Scientifically speaking, I'll just need to keep my centre of gravity on the right side of the ledge. And of course I mustn't look down. I'll look at the buzzards.

He takes one end of the rope, attaches the caribina to his belt loop and starts to climb over the edge of the scaff. tower.

Titty: Will he really be able to do it? I couldn't do it, and I know Roger couldn't.

Roger: I could!

Dot: He'll be alright. Dick, don't forget where you are!

Titty: I wish John was here.

Dick: Right, I'm off. Don't come too near the edge. If I slip I don't want you to be dragged over.

He sets off very slowly down the front of the scaff. tower.
Dot: Are you alright?

Dick: So far!

Dot: You're not giddy?

Dick: No! I just need to think about my centre of gravity!

Titty: Is he alright?

Dot: As long as he keeps talking like that, yes!

Dick: I'm nearly at the sheep.

Dick reaches the level of the sheep and sits down on the bar. The sheep suddenly moves a lot and bleats loudly. Dick is startled and nearly falls off.

RANSOME CENTRE STAGE

Dick: Aaargh!

Roger: Are you all right?

Dick: Yes. I just need to keep calm. I don't want the sheep to get frightened and wriggle off the ledge.

He strokes the sheep and starts to wrap the rope around the front legs of the sheep.

Dick: A red spot. It's one of Mr Dixon's. (*to himself*) I hope none of those sailors notice my terrible knot. I wish I knew how to do it properly.

He knots the rope. The puppeteer makes a bleating sound and lets the sheep go.

Dick: Right. That's the best I can do. The poor thing is frozen and terrified. Lower away!

Titty: Lower away!

Titty, Dot and Roger start to lower the sheep gently down the tower. John, Susan and Peggy appear from stage right pulling the sledge. They notice what's happening on the crag and rush to the base.

Roger: Here come the dogs!

Dick: (*talking to himself*) John's going to see my useless knot.

Susan: They're not fit to be left alone for a minute!

Peggy: Why are there only three of them?

John: Don't shout! Dick's halfway up the cliff without a rope. Don't startle him.

Susan: What on earth are they doing?

Peggy: Cragfast sheep! Good for them! Whoever owns it

will be jolly pleased.

The sheep reaches the bottom. John looks at the knot but says nothing. He unties the rope then gently lifts the sheep onto the sledge. Peggy and Susan wrap it up in a coat.

Susan: How is he going to get down?

Dick: I'll just wriggle my way along the ledge.

John: That'll take ages. Stay put. I'll get up there and lower you down in two shakes. Pull the rope up and tie it round you.

John runs and climbs up the scaff. tower. Dick looks down and has a wobble.

Dick: Woah! Time to look at the buzzards I think!

John reaches the top of the scaff. tower.

John: Have you tied the knot?

Dick: Yes!

John: Ready when you are.

Dick: (*takes a deep breath*) Ready now.

John starts to pretend to lower Dick down. Dick climbs down the front of the scaff. tower, making it look as if tension on the rope is lowering him

Dick: I just need to concentrate on my centre of gravity! And those buzzards. And I do believe that might be a nest!

Susan: He's not looking down! He's staring up at the crags!

Peggy: He's jolly brave.

Dick reaches the bottom

Dick: Oh! I'm down!

Peggy: Well done! Jolly good work! And the sheep's still alive. We may be in time to save it but it's pretty bad.

Dick: (*untying the rope*) What do buzzards make their nests out of?

Peggy: (*startled, confused*) Any old sticks!

Dick: Thought so (*he pulls a notebook and pencil out of his pocket, blows on his frozen fingers and writes in his book*) "saw buzzard's nest".

Peggy and Susan look at each other quizzically.

John: (*calls*) Heads!

He throws down the rope. He, Titty, Roger and Dot climb down the side of the scaff. tower. Everyone pats Dick on the back then gather round the sheep.

Peggy: It's starving. It may have been up there for days.

Roger: Have some chocolate, sheepy.

He tries to give the sheep some chocolate but it shows no interest (one of the actors has squatted down and is acting as the sheep's puppeteer)

Peggy: Farmers would give it some warm milk.

Susan: But we haven't got any.

Dick: It's got a red mark on its shoulder. That means it belongs to Mr Dixon.

John: We'd better take it back to him as quick as we can.

Susan: We'll bump it to death going over these rocks.

Peggy: I know an old road that goes straight down through the woods. The charcoal-burners use it. Come on!

Titty, Roger and Dot take up the ropes of the sledge. Just before Dick takes up a rope, John pats him the shoulder and smiles.

John: Well done, that man.

Dick: (*going pink*) Thank you!

They all set off.

Peggy: Well this is a funny sort-of crossing of Greenland. Coming back with a sick sheep.

Titty: Let's just say it's a polar bear.

Dick: Hi Dot. I saw the buzzards nest!

Dot: I'm glad. I really am.

They all exit stage left.

SCENE 11 – DIXONS, COFFIN/SLEDGE

Enter Old Silas pushing his barrow and Mr Dixon, who removes the white sheet from the windows. They look up as the children enter pulling the sledge as fast as they can. They stop in front of the farmers, out of breath.

Old Silas: Well bless me, what's this Dixon?

Peggy: Cragfast sheep!

The farmers squat down. One of the children acts as the puppeteer for the sheep as the farmers stroke it gently.

Old Silas: It's a near thing. Another night and she'd have been a goner. Where did you find her?

Peggy: Up on the crag above the charcoal-burners' wood. She was stuck on a ledge halfway up the cliff.

Old Silas: And how in ever did you get her down out of that?

Titty: Dick did it. He climbed down to the ledge while we stayed at the top with the rope.

Old Silas: It's not the first sheep to come crag fast there, but it's a bad spot to get them out of without men and ropes.

Titty: Dick tied the rope to the sheep and we lowered her down.

A pause. Dixon then stands up and looks Dick in the face for the first time.

Dixon: Well I'm beholden to you all. There's not many lads would climb down to that ledge.

Everyone is startled. This is the most Dixon has ever said in front of them. Then Mrs Dixon enters.

Mrs Dixon: Look at him! He's wet-through! And frozen! Get up those stairs and get out of those clothes! Arctic indeed! He'll have more'n enough of Arctic standing there in wet breeches watching you nurse a sick sheep. Get in lad!

Dick rushes off stage right.

Mrs Dixon: Right, come on in the rest of you and warm yourselves by the fire. I've a rare baking of cakes. Silas'll set you on the road with a lantern when you've warmed up.

Silas leads the sledge offstage left. Mr Dixon sets out the table and everyone gathers around it. Silas comes back in and he and Dixon sit to one side as the others talk.

Mrs Dixon: So, tell me all about it!

Susan: It was Dick who was the real hero!

The children mime an excited discussion as Dixon and Old Silas look at each other and walk out of the kitchen. They go off stage left and pull out the sledge and look over it.

Mr Dixon: We might do worse.

Old Silas: It's not such a job as we can't tackle it.

They walk off stage left. Music covers the other children striking their chairs, taking their rucksacks and setting off home. The lights lower. Silas enters stage left with a lantern and leads the children off stage left. He returns and stands at the stage left door, holding his lantern up, casting the light into the dressing room. Dot goes up to the scaff. tower where Dick is wearing his pyjamas. Mrs Dixon tidies the kitchen, closes the doors and takes the table off stage right. The music fades out to the sound of sawing wood (played on the violin). The light drops to one spot on the scaff. tower and Silas's lantern.

Dot: Dick! Do you hear that saw? The sheep's died after all. I can hear them in the barn, making the coffin.

Dick: (*calling out of the window to Old Silas*) Is the sheep alright?

Silas: (*calls back*) Doing fine.

Mrs Dixon: (*offstage*) YOU TWO! BED!!

Dot and Dick jump back from the window and there is a blackout.

SCENE 12 – THE FRAM

Outside Holly Howe, Peggy, John, Susan, Roger, Titty and the Doctor

Doctor: Are you sure they know to come here?

Peggy: We put up the right signal. "Come to Holly Howe". They've never been late before.

John: Bother those Ds.

Roger: Here they come!

The Ds enter on their sledge (somehow!)

John: Where did you get the sledge?

Dick: Mr Dixon made it, after we helped the sheep.

They all gather around the sledge and admire it.

John: It's a fine sledge!

Titty: How is the sheep?

Dorothea: Much better. Mrs Dixon has got it in the kitchen and is feeding it warm milk. It should be better in a couple of weeks.

Doctor: Right. I can't hang around all day, this is just a quick visit for an inspection.

OTLEY – WINTER HOLIDAY

Dorothea: How's Nancy?

Doctor: As well as can be expected. (*He puffs out his cheeks and shows her pumpkin face with his hands*)

They all laugh

Doctor: Very good. Nobody's holding their jaw. If you can laugh like that, there's not much wrong with you.

He starts to leave, then remembers something

Doctor: Oh yes, there is something. (*He pulls a small parcel out of his pocket*).

Peggy: A message from Nancy?

Doctor: I don't think it's a message exactly. (*shakes the parcel and sound of metal on metal*) Doesn't sound like one. She is a masterful young woman, that Nancy of yours. Why, I told her there was no way I could bring anything for you. But before I quite knew what had happened… well, here it is.

Peggy takes the parcel

Peggy: (*reading*) "Don't open until he's gone. He knows why."

Doctor: She offered to show it me, but I said I'd rather know nothing about it. Your Uncle Jim gave me some advice years ago, and I don't think Nancy grows safer with age…

Roger: What is it?

Doctor: Don't open it until he's gone. And he's going. All I can say is that it's free of mumps, as you can see from the singeing. See you in a few days.

All: Bye

Doctor exits

John: Let's open it up.

There's a tobacco tin inside the parcel. They open that and pull out a large key. There is a large label on the key. Peggy reads it.

Peggy: "Fram"

Susan: What does that mean?

John: The *Fram* was Nansen's ship, that was frozen in the ice…

Peggy: Of course! I remember Uncle Jim reading about it. They went into the ice on purpose and drifted across the Arctic…

John: But what's the key?

Peggy: It's the key of the houseboat.

General sharp intake of breath

Roger: So we can get inside?

Titty: Not while Captain Flint's away.

Peggy: Why not? Think of it. A ship, frozen in the ice… He always leaves a key at Beckfoot while he's away. Sometimes Mother takes us across and we open the windows and give the cabin an airing.

John: It is bad for a ship to be left shut up for a long time and not be properly aired.

Peggy: There you go then…

Susan: But are you sure Captain Flint would want us

going in his cabin?

Peggy: He'd be jolly pleased. Oh come on! What's the key for? Skates on.

They all mime putting on skates and set off across the lake towards the Fram. *They arrive at the side of the boat*

Titty: It's awfully like burgling…

Peggy: He's my uncle!

John: I wonder if he knows she's frozen in. Okay, skates off.

They mime removing their skates. They all climb aboard. Peggy fits the key into the lock but struggles to open it.

Susan: Perhaps it's the wrong key? We mustn't force the lock.

Dick: Probably some water's got in the lock and frozen.

John: I bet that's what's the matter.

Suddenly it turns and they open up.

Susan: Well it certainly does need airing. And we should open the curtains and let some sunlight in.

Titty: Of course he's away. But doesn't it feel as if there were somebody here?

Susan: I think I'll open the door in the fo'c'sle and get a draught right through… And perhaps I ought to light the stove…

Dick: (*looking through some books*) Here it is. *Farthest North – the voyage of the* Fram. This will tell us everything we need to know. And there's another about Lord Franklin and the North-West Passage.

Roger: (*looking at something off stage, in the* Fram) He's got a tremendous lot of good stores. Jam. Corned Beef. Sardines.

Susan: Shut that cupboard door, Roger.

A speeded up section showing that several days are spent on the Fram. *Coming and going. Arriving with sheepskin rugs from Mr Dixon. Starting to eat the jam, the corned beef and the sardines... Lights coming up and down to show days passing quickly – Northwest Passage excerpt sung over this. Day and night done with coming and going and lights going up and down.*
One day... back on the ice

Roger: A sail!

They all look out across the auditorium.

Peggy: It's one of the ice yachts.

John, Susan, Roger, Titty and Peggy spellbound. Dick and Dot interested.

Dorothea: It's very pretty.

John: (*breathlessly*) She'll have to go about. But how can she?

Titty and Roger: She's gone about.

Dick: How does it work?

Roger: Tacking

Dick: How?

Titty: If it was summer, we'd show you.

John: She's going so fast!

They mime watching her woosh past

Titty: Couldn't we put a sail on a sledge? The whole lake's frozen now so there's no fear of sailing off the edge…

Roger: Nansen did it.

Dick: Yes, I saw the picture. A square sail.

John: Yes – his wouldn't have tacked. But – it might be possible. The *Swallow*'s old mast and sail are in the boathouse.

Peggy: It's worth a go.

Dick: *Fram* again tomorrow?

Susan: Yes. The cabin still needs some airing…

SCENE 13 – SAILING SLEDGE

Dick and Dorothea arrive at the Fram but the door is locked. They leave their things "on deck" and move away.

They look out across the lake.

Dick: There's the ice yacht again.

Dorothea: What's that? There's another one. A very small one, with a brown sail.

Dick: I've left my telescope in my knapsack

Dorothea: I do believe it's them!

Dick: It can't be!

Dorothea: It's a sledge.

Dick: It is them! They've got the yellow flag on the masthead.

Roger: (*offstage*) Hi!

Dick and Dorothea: Hello!

Dorothea: Look out, they're coming right for us!

Peggy: (*offstage*) Shove your port legs down. HARD!

Sound of crashing and tumbling. John, Susan, Roger, Titty and Peggy enter in a heap, including a mast and sail

Dick and Dorothea run up to them

Dorothea: Are you all right?

John: No damage done. The mast hasn't broken

Susan: Anybody hurt?

Roger: Usual knees... But not too bad.

Susan: Peggy have you cut yourself? Come on into the *Fram*. There's lint and iodine in the cupboard.

Peggy: I think a skate cut through my glove...

Susan: Come on then... Watch her, Dot, I think Peggy's going to faint.

Peggy: I jolly well am not! Shiver my timbers! Reach into my pocket, Dot, for the key.

Most go into the Fram. *Dick and John remain on the ice.*

Dick: But why did it turn over?

John: Too narrow. She was fine until we tried reaching – that's when you have the wind blowing from one side. Trouble is, you can't really steer her... You turning sailor?

OTLEY – WINTER HOLIDAY

Dick: I'd like to know how it works

John: Come in, I'll draw a diagram.

Peggy: Show Dick and Dot the picture.

John: Of course. I nearly forgot. Nancy has sent a picture, but we can't make head nor tail of it.

John pulls out a sheet of paper and the others gather round

Titty: Look. There we all are on the sledge. Seven of us. And we're following the sign to the North Pole. I'm sure she means we're to go straight away.

Peggy: But why? The weather's holding and she'll be able to come with us soon.

Dick: The people in the crowd look like the semaphore drawings Nancy drew for me.

John: He's got it.

Peggy: Galoots we are! Donks! Of course that's what they're doing…

John *is already writing the letters down*

John: But it doesn't make sense…

Peggy: Marfeht nignip eels siohw?

Titty: Do you two have your own language?

Peggy: Not yet…

Titty: What about the signpost? Should we read the letters the other way?

Peggy: You've got it. It's a jolly good thing Nancy doesn't know how long it took us to work it out. "Who is slee… Who is sleeping in the *Fram*?"

John: But nobody is!

Roger: Unless there have been burglars?

Peggy: But we've been here every day and have always locked up. Oh…

John: What?

Peggy: She doesn't mean somebody has been sleeping in the *Fram*. She's asking which of us is sleeping here.

Susan: But none of us are.

Peggy: But she thinks we should be. We would be if she wasn't ill.

Susan: If she wasn't ill we'd be at school.

Peggy: You know what I mean. Here we are with a *Fram* to sleep in, much warmer than our own bedrooms. It really does get very warm with the stove on all day. And Nancy's always saying that the worst thing about the Winter Holiday is that you can't get away from the house at night. That's why she's thought of it…

Susan: But…

John: Peggy's right. That's just what Nancy means.

Susan: But we can't really.

Roger: Why not?

Titty: Let's all sleep aboard tonight.

Susan: Well you won't anyway. Either of you.

Peggy: But you and John can.

Dorothea: It would be a lovely thing to do.

Peggy: We simply can't let Nancy down. We've got to!

John: I just don't know.

Titty, Roger, Dick and Dorothea exit into the Fram, *John, Susan and Peggy skate a little way away.*

John: It does feel awfully as though Nancy has dared us to do it. I wouldn't like to say "no".

Susan: As long as those two brats get to bed at the proper time...

Peggy: Three million cheers, Susan...

Susan: I haven't said yes. Not yet...

Blackout

SCENE 14 – NIGHT ON THE FRAM

Enter John, Susan and Peggy carrying rucksacks, walking in the dark with torches – blue-out.

John: Right. Mr & Mrs Jackson set off to watch the play in Rio ages ago. We need to get a move on.

Susan: Look here, are you sure this is a good idea? I know Mother would think the *Fram* would be no place for us at night.

Peggy: It's too good a plan to waste!

They start walking on the spot, facing the audience.

Peggy: Shiver my timbers! A real smuggling night. Isn't it a pity Nancy isn't here?

Susan: We may meet Mrs Jackson coming home.

Peggy: No chance. Nancy'll never believe we've done it!

John: We'll start back as soon as it's light.

Susan: We'll meet the Jacksons milking when we come in.

Peggy: Who cares? Jib-booms and bobstays! We'll have done it then! And anyhow, we're not doing anything wrong.

John and Susan look at each other. They turn and look back at the windows in the moonlight. They are lit up with a dim white light. They all cheer up.

John: The *Fram*!

Susan: Oh she does look fine in the moonlight!

John: Pretty gorgeous. Come on!

They mime putting their skates on and skate up to the Fram, *covered by music. They mime climbing on board.*

Peggy: Let's get in and get the stove on.

They open the windows wide and settle into the Fram.

John: Look here, we simply can't go to bed right away. Shall we cook something?

Susan: What about cocoa?

Peggy: Good idea.

Peggy and Susan start boiling the kettle and John settles down to read an astronomy book. Slowly they start to look from one to the other. They all look unhappy.

Peggy: Isn't that beastly kettle ever going to boil?

Pause.

Susan: It's no good. John and I have just got to go back.

We can't leave Titty and Roger alone all night. But you'll be alright, if you want to stay. You can lock yourself in.

Peggy: But that isn't what Nancy wants. She wants us all to be here.

Susan: Well we can't. John thinks just the same.

John nods sadly.

John: Anyway, we've been here in the dark, and in the real Arctic it's dark all the time in Winter.

Susan: Don't let's bother with this wretched cocoa. We'll have it when we come in the morning.

Pause

Peggy: I suppose Nancy will be pleased that we've come here by moonlight, but she'll think the *Fram*'s wasted all the same. Come on then.

They pick up their bags, sort out the kettle and close/lock up the Fram. *They put on their skates and get back down on to the ice.*

John: Hullo, what's that?

Enter Titty and Roger stage right holding torches.

Susan: (*dismayed*) It isn't! Yes it is. It's those two brats. We never should have gone out!

Titty: The light's out in the houseboat. They must have gone to sleep.

Roger: Let's give them a shout!

Roger/Titty: *Fram* ahoy!

John: (*annoyed*) Hullo.

Roger: There's something moving on the ice! Bears!

Titty: It's them!

Susan: What on earth are you two doing out here? We left you tucked up in bed!

Titty: We were coming to the *Fram*.

Susan: You ought to have stayed in bed. We're on our way home.

Roger: But what did you go there for?

Titty: We thought you'd gone there to sleep.

Susan: Quick march! You ought to be asleep now. Let's get off the ice and back to Holly Howe as fast as we can.

They take off their skates and start walking back. Enter Mr & Mrs Jackson.

John: It's the Jacksons!

Peggy: Oh no!

Susan: Hurry up!

The dog howls.

Mrs Jackson: Eh, what's this? And you not in bed! This is no time for walking, grand night though it is. What would your mothers say if they knew?

Peggy: We'll be in bed in two minutes.

Peggy, John and Susan run off stage right.

Roger: Why did the dog howl like that?

Mr Jackson: Got a friend in the moon likely.

Titty: Did you have a nice time at the party?

Mrs Jackson: Well I never did hear the beat of that! Off to bed the pair of you!

Titty and Roger scoot off stage right.

Mrs Jackson: Ee, but I don't wonder people can't sleep these nights with all the noise they make skating in the bay.

Exit.

SCENE 15 – CAPTAIN FLINT ABROAD, NORTH STAR

In a port somewhere in Europe (France perhaps?) enter Captain Flint and a newspaper salesman with a hoarding saying "Great Frost: England's largest lake frozen end to end"

Captain Flint: I'll take a paper, thank you. (*takes paper*) Merci beaucoup. This takes me back. When I was a school boy the lake back home froze like that. Ice yachts, ice fishing, figure-skating and curling… I think it's definitely time to head home.

Song: North Star

SCENE 16 – Ds ALONE/CAPTAIN FLINT RETURNS

Dick and Dorothea skate up to the Fram. The others are all sitting "on the Fram".

Dick: I wonder if they stayed there last night?

Dorothea: I think they were going to. The older ones.

Dick: Look, there's the ice yacht again. (*They watch it across the auditorium*). It doesn't turn over like the sledge because it's much wider. But I wish I knew how it can sail against the wind.

Dorothea: (*to the others*) Hello!

Swallows and Peggy: Hi!

Roger: We were here in the middle of the night!

Dorothea: Susan never let you sleep here?

Titty: No. But we did come out onto the ice. A long time after bed time.

Dorothea: What was it like in the dark?

Peggy: We had to go home to sleep.

Susan: It couldn't be helped.

John: It was a sort of promise we'd made to Mother. And Titty and Roger are so very young...

Susan: As it was they were out very late...

Dorothea: (*surprised by these excuses!*) But what are you going to say to Nancy?

The three older ones look at each other uncomfortably

Peggy: She'll be as sick as anything.

Susan: It can't be helped. Nancy'd understand if she were here.

John: No she wouldn't. Not really. But it can't be helped all the same.

Peggy: What about you two? You haven't promised anything to anybody? And you're as much part of the expedition as anybody else. Why, even Nancy said so. You sleep in her. Nancy'd be as pleased as anything!

Dorothea: But... but she didn't mean us when she sent the picture!

Peggy: Of course she did!

Titty: She drew all seven of us...

Peggy: Gosh! I mean, shiver my timbers! What does it matter who sleeps here as long as it's someone? Of course, if you'd rather not...

Dick: Oh let's! It would be even better than the observatory for looking at stars.

Dorothea: (*to Peggy*) What about you?

Peggy: I'll sleep here too, if you will. (*Suddenly looks between John and Susan and Dick and Dorothea uncertainly*) Look here. Let her be your ship tonight, so we can send Nancy an answer. And I'll come here tomorrow night, if you want me.

Dorothea: We'd simply love to!

John: I wish we could.

Peggy: Come on, let's write an answer for Nancy.

Dick: Semaphore? Like hers?

Peggy: Just two Ds. I know, let's do it at Holly Howe and try and catch the doctor before he goes to Rio. Let's let the Ds move in to the *Fram* and make it home.

John: All right. We'll see you two tomorrow.

Peggy: Here's the key. (*Hands Dorothea the key*)

Susan: Can you work the stove?

Dorothea: Yes.

John, Peggy, Susan, Titty and Roger all start to leave

Titty: Good luck!

Peggy: Hurrah for the Ds.

Dorothea: Goodbye!

Dick and Dot left alone on the ice.

Dorothea: It's almost like they ran away!

Dick: What? It's a good job I left my astronomy book here yesterday.

Dorothea: Yes. What a story I could write about this. Two in the Ice. "Wake up Professor, another day in the ice…"

Dick: Shall we get in and light the stove?

Dorothea: You go in. I'm going to read for a while.

Dick goes "into the Fram". Dorothea sits down and picks up her book and starts to read. The lights change to suggest time passing.

Blackout. A spot comes on the top of the tower where

OTLEY – WINTER HOLIDAY

Nancy sits up in bed with a sheet of paper in her hands – it will have two big semaphore letter Ds on it

Nancy: Well shiver my timbers! The Ds, sleeping in the Fram!

A door slams. Voices chatter.

Nancy: Mother! Who was that?!

Mother: (*off stage*) It was your Uncle Jim! I sent him packing. Don't worry, he's gone to the houseboat to sleep.

Nancy: To the houseboat???... Oh...!!! (*collapses into horrified laughter*)

Lights comes back up on Dorothea

Dorothea puts her book down and looks out across the "ice".

Enter Captain Flint, towing a sledge and heading towards the Fram

Dorothea: (*to Dick*) There's a man out there with a sledge. He looks like a picture from that book about Holland that Father had...

Dick: What?

Dorothea: The tall Dutchman bowed low. (putting on Dutch accent) "Madam, your taste in tulips has become proverbial in my country..." I really do like them. "and I have come from..." Where should a tall Dutchman come from? "I have come from Amsterdam to offer you a small collection." Skates and Tulips by Dorothea Callum...

Captain Flint arrives at the Fram. *Dorothea looks taken aback as he puts his suitcase on the "deck". He is staring at her in great surprise.*

Dorothea: I'm sorry, but who are you?
Captain Flint: I beg your pardon?!
Dorothea: I'm really not sure we should let you onboard…
Captain Flint: Well, I'm jiggered!

INTERVAL

OTLEY – WINTER HOLIDAY

ACT TWO

SCENE 1 – THE MORNING AFTER

John, Susan, Roger, Titty and Peggy skate up towards the Fram. Smoke drifts up from above the Fram *(the stove)*

Peggy: Hurray! They did stay there. I was half afraid they might have thought better of it. Come on.

They skate closer

John: What's that notice?

A large sign is on the side of the Fram. *It reads* "TRESPASSERS will be hanged – like the last"

Roger: Trespassers will be hanged…. Like the last!

Peggy: What cheek!

Titty: Perhaps some seals have been trying to come aboard again.

Peggy: Cheek all the same, to put up a notice like that. It's all very well Nancy doing something like that, but not the Ds!

John: Well, they were in charge…

They mime removing their skates.

John: Morning you two!

No answer

Susan: They'll have got hungry and gone off to Dixon's Farm for breakfast, without waiting for us.

Titty: That's why they've put the notice up

John: Not a bad idea really, although "hanged" is a bit much...

Peggy rattles the door

Peggy: Bother them! It's locked. They've gone for milk and taken the key!

Susan: We'll just have to wait for them.

There are sounds from inside the Fram

Peggy: Listen. Sh!

There's another sound

Peggy: (rattling the door again) Hi! Buck up and let us in! (*a pause*) Don't be donks! We'll drop icicles down the chimney and smoke you out! This isn't funny at all.

The Fram *door opens and Captain Flint emerges. Everybody quite startled*

Titty: Hello! It's Captain Flint!

Captain Flint: Hello Able Seaman! Hello Skipper, Mate, Ship's Boy. But I say, Peggy, why haven't you been keeping an eye on things. Somebody's got in here while I've been away and turned the place upside down. And eaten all the stores.

Peggy: Umm...

Captain Flint: And that's not the worst of it! I caught some of them in the very act. They've been living here! A boy and a girl – utter strangers of course – all set up to camp down for the night. Well it didn't take long to settle them...

Peggy: But Uncle Jim, it's all of us! Well, Nancy and me at any rate. We thought you'd be glad to have the place properly aired while you were away…

Captain Flint: You mean to say it was you who got in here and made such a terrible mess?

John: It wasn't Peggy alone. It was all of us.

Susan: We were going to make everything perfectly tidy again before we left…

Captain Flint fights back a smile

Captain Flint: Well I suppose I could have trusted you to see to that, Susan. But I think you might have made sure the door was properly locked at night! You must have left the key in the lock or that pair of burgling scallywags would never have dared to break in. Well they won't go burgling again in a hurry, I can tell you that…

John: But it was our fault they were here. They would never have come if we hadn't brought them.

Peggy: (*angrily*) They were our friends! We left them here ourselves! What have you done with them?

Captain Flint: You read the notice, didn't you? They were the last…

Roger: But he can't have hanged them! He's probably got them locked in the fo'c'sle…

Titty: Well he should let them out at once.

Captain Flint: Too late now. How could I tell they were friends of yours?

Roger squeezes past Captain Flint into the Fram

Peggy: So you turned them out? It's the beastliest thing you've ever done! It wasn't their fault at all, and Dorothea would never understand why you were being so beastly...

Roger re-emerges.

Roger: They aren't here.

Captain Flint: Of course they aren't.

Peggy: If you've done anything horrid to them, we'll never speak to you again. I don't care that we made a mess of your boat. You don't deserve a boat. I'm sorry we didn't make a bigger mess! You wait till Nancy hears about this...

Enter Dick and Dorothea

Dorothea: Hello! Hi Susan, has he already had his breakfast? Mrs Dixon's sent some rashers of bacon in case he's forgotten to get any.

They all stare at Dick and Dorothea as if they are ghosts

Peggy: Look here, Dorothea. Was he beastly? What did happen when he turned up?

Dorothea: We had tea. And then they looked at the stars...

Peggy: (*to Captain Flint*) Then why did you pretend to be such a beast?

Captain Flint: (*Smiling*) Well you gave me quite a surprise last night. I thought one deserved another. Anyway, are you coming aboard?

They all climb aboard

Captain Flint: After a bit of tea, I think I'll go and see the real culprit and find out what she's really up to...

Peggy: But Nancy's been very ill…

Captain Flint: Oh I know. I got turfed out of Beckfoot the moment I arrived last night. Don't worry, I won't forget that she's had a face like a water-melon…

Roger: Pumpkin!

Captain Flint: Pumpkin if you prefer. But I don't doubt she's had a hand in things, sickbed or not.

Music covers – Captain Flint exits skating, others do speeded up tidying up in the **Fram**. *Sit somewhere else.*

SCENE 2 – USES OF AN UNCLE/FRAM/NANCY RECOVERING

Over music, they start tidying the Fram. *Enter Captain Flint skating across the ice towing a sledge with a full sack on it.*

Captain Flint: Ahoy The Fram!

All the children: (*excited*) Did you see Nancy?

Captain Flint: I did. Very disappointing. I must have arrived too late to see her in full bloom. Her face is no bigger than usual.

Titty: Did you talk to her?

Captain Flint: Yes, but in Semaphore, from the far end of the lawn!

Peggy: We're not even allowed to do that! Well? What did she say?

Captain Flint: Well she was worried about what happened when I met Dick and Dot! Ha! But mostly we talked about the North Pole. I need to have a talk with the people who own it, and get hold of the key.

Dick: Key? A key to the North Pole?

Peggy: Wait and see!

John: And what about Nancy herself?

Captain Flint: The doctor says she can pull down the plague flag in a week's time and meet up with the rest of us.

Titty: And we've got ten days before we have to go back to school!

Susan: Unless somebody else gets mumps.
Everyone feels their jaws.
Captain Flint: So with a bit of luck, the full expedition is on. Unless it starts to thaw of course. At the first sign on any thaw we'll have to set off straight away.

Exit Peggy

Everyone looks anxiously at the sky. Lights change and music (a song? 'I'm Already There' – Chris Leslie?) covers a 'montage' to show time passing by –this is coupled with scenes of Captain Flint buying stores from a shop in one stage light and Nancy practising walking with Mrs Blackett in another spot near the scaff. tower. Music fades out and everyone exits apart from Swallows and Ds who have changed places.

OTLEY – WINTER HOLIDAY

Titty: The days are just dragging by! I can't wait to be off!

John: There's no sign of a thaw at least. It's freezing harder and harder.

Enter Peggy

Peggy: News from Captain Flint! We've got to make sure we're really ready! Nancy's been exercising like mad and is feeling loads better. It could be any day now!

All: HURRAH!

John: (*stand*) And when we get the call to set off we'll all just go from wherever we are when we see the signal. It's not a race – and anyway it's not fair to expect Nancy to skate all the way down here to the *Fram* first.

Titty: (*stand*) First group to get to the Pole will raise a flag.

Dick: But what if we don't know the Pole when we see it?

Peggy: Honestly, you'd know it straight away. It's right up at the head of the lake, the extreme north of the Arctic, only a few yards off the ice. Trust me, you can't miss it.

Enter Captain Flint towing a loaded sledge

Captain Flint: Hullo you lot! Right, I'm off on a long journey, but I'll be back by tea-time, and I'll be starving so make sure something's ready!

Roger: Which way are you going? Do you need some dogs to help pull the sledge?

Captain Flint: Thanks. But not this time.

He skates off slowly, pulling the heavy sledge and exits

Roger: Let's go after him!

Peggy: Rot! And anyway, we need to get ready!

Dick: Actually, we'd better get back to Dixon's.

Roger: What for?

Dick looks very bothered.
Dorothea: It's something he's got to do.

Titty: Secret?

Dick: It's for the expedition.

Susan: Leave him alone you two!

Dorothea: Come on. See you all soon!

Dick and Dot start skating towards the audience and end up skating in a spot as the rest of the stage falls to darkness. Come to audience.
Dick: Thanks Dot. I really didn't want to tell them, in case it doesn't work.

Dorothea: A pleasure. And I really think it will work. Mr Dixon is ever so clever.

Dick: Just think, a mast and sail of our very own.

Dorothea: For our very own sailing sledge! We'll be much faster than the others.

Dick: You sound like Mr Dixon! It's not a competition!

Exit Dick and Dot – skate off left. Blackout.
Lights up on Swallows and Peggy at the Fram. *Enter a tired looking Captain Flint with an empty sledge.*
Roger: He's back! And the box has gone!

Peggy: Don't ask him where he's been!

Susan: How many lumps of sugar in your tea?

Captain Flint: By Jove, I'm so thirsty I could drink it with

40 in! Let's say 3 to be on the safe side! What's become of those Ds?

(Susan goes right to make tea)

John: Busy at home.

Peggy: Up to something.

Captain Flint: Well we need them to come to the *Fram* tomorrow.

John: I'll put a signal up as soon as we get back tonight.

Captain Flint: Good….. because they're going to let Nancy loose on the world tomorrow.

All the children go mad!

Captain Flint: Woah there!

Roger: Three million cheers!!

Peggy: Don't be such a galoot! Shut up!

Captain Flint: We don't know what time tomorrow as there will have to be disinfection, fumigation and so forth. Not before 12 at any rate. So, after the doctor's been, Nancy'll raise a flag on the promontory – a white one means hang on till the next day, a red one means she'll be able to come over and have dinner with us here.

John: But what about the pole?

Captain Flint: We'll have a full council as soon as Nancy can come over, then get going. Probably the day after tomorrow.

All: Hooray!

Blackout.

In the blackout, enter Dick and Mr Dixon with their sledge. Mr Dixon is fiddling with the mast and sail.

Mr Dixon: Hi there Dick, may I see the drawing in your notebook? I can't remember how we were going to step the mast.

Dick fishes out his notebook and hands it to Mr Dixon, who flicks through it.

Mr Dixon: Ah! Signals! I learned Semaphore in the army. What's this? 'Flag at Beckfoot = start for Pole'?

Dick: That's the signal we're waiting for! As soon as we see a flag on the Beckfoot promontory, we have to start the expedition.

Mr Dixon: Right, I see! Then we'd better get moving with this here mast! We can't have them lot at Jackson's going faster than thee!

Blackout. Music.

SCENE 3 – FLAG AT BECKFOOT (OBSERVATORY)

Dick and Dot at the foot of the scaffold.

Dorothea: I saw them leave ages ago. We're awfully late.

Dick: Come to *Fram*. Thought so. (He scans the horizon with his telescope. Suddenly he freezes. Gasps. He starts scrabbling for his pocket book.)

Dorothea: What is it?

Dick: There's a flag at Beckfoot. A huge one. No wonder the others looked in such a rush.

Dorothea: Why?

Dick shows Dorothea the important page in his pocketbook

Dick: "Flag at Beckfoot equals Start for Pole". I wrote it down when Nancy told me.

Dorothea: But that means they've got the wrong signal up.

Dick: They've just left it up from yesterday, like ours. Hold on.

Dick hoists up North Cone over Diamond

Dick: There we go. Come to North Pole. Now come on, quick. We've got to try and catch them up. I'm glad we've got our mast and sail. Come on!

Blackout.

SCENE 4 – COUNCIL AT THE FRAM (PART 1)

John, Susan, Roger, Titty, Peggy and Captain Flint sit in the Fram – they have changed position.

Peggy: Bother those Ds. They ought to be keel-hauled and hung from the yard arm. Being late for a council…

Titty: But they don't know it's a council.

Captain Flint: You sure you put the right signal up?

John: Oh yes.

Susan: Remember they were doing something for the expedition. Perhaps they didn't get it finished?

Captain Flint: Nancy won't be here till about 1 o'clock… But perhaps someone should go and stir them up?

John: I'll go.

Captain Flint: Good man. I want us all here before Nancy comes. We could go and meet her part of the way, and we want a good crowd to give her a cheer.

John: I'll have them here in two shakes.

Exit John stage left

Titty: So what's Nancy doing this morning?

Captain Flint: I gather there's some tremendous disinfection to be done. She will probably smell like a chemist's shop when she gets here.

Roger: Shall I keep a lookout?

Captain Flint: Why not? Now is somebody going to help me with this plum pudding?

Roger starts back but Captain Flint ushers him away

Susan: I will.

Titty: So what's going to happen tomorrow then?

Captain Flint: That's what we're going to discuss at the council! And much of it's a secret anyway…

Peggy: What can you tell us?

Captain Flint: Well it's all decided that we'll go in three separate parties. We'll all rush off as fast as we can to the Pole, and the first there will hoist a flag. (*louder*) Any sign of them yet Roger?

Enter Roger
Roger: What?
Captain Flint: Just wondered if there was any sign of John and those Ds?
Roger: Oh right…

There are sounds outside. Lighting changes to indicate a storm brewing.
Roger: Here's someone… It's getting very dark out there, by the way.
Captain Flint: Dark? At this time?
Enter John
John: They're not at the farm. Are they here?
Captain Flint: No.
John: Just come and look at the sky.
Captain Flint walks over and looks out.
Captain Flint: That's snow. I think it's going to be heavy. Let's hope wherever those two are they have the sense to stay there.

SCENE 5 – RACE FOR THE POLE

Dorothea and Dick walk across the stage with sledge – mast up, sail furled.

Dick: Mrs Jackson said that they all left in a rush when they saw Nancy's flag.

Dorothea: That means they'll be an awfully long way ahead. Come on. (*She hands Dick another rope*)

Dick: Shall we let the sail down?

Dorothea: There isn't much wind at the moment. Let's keep going.

They pull the sledge together

Dorothea: It looks like people are stopping skating. What's the matter?

Dick: Where's the sun gone?

They turn around – wind noise.

Dorothea: Look at that! The islands are disappearing. It's… it's snow…

Starts to snow. Smoke machine, fans on and scraps of paper flying.

Dick: There's a wind coming with it. I can feel it. Let's get the sail ready.

They unfurl the sail and sit on the sledge. At first nothing happens.

Dorothea: If it doesn't work we'll just have to go back to pulling it…

Dick: The wind's strengthening…

The sail is pulled out on a string to indicate it is filling with wind.

Dorothea: So's the snow…

OTLEY – WINTER HOLIDAY

Dick: She's moving!

Dick and Dot cling to the sledge to indicate it's moving fast. The sledge is illuminated in a single spot to help with the suggestion of movement, sound effect of runners on ice.

Dorothea: Watch out for your mitten, Dick… (*Dick's mitten falls from the sledge and is pulled away fast on a string to demonstrate it being left behind)* Oh Dick!

Dick: Can't be helped.

Dorothea: We're going so fast!

Dick: Wonderful isn't it?

Dorothea: But where are we?

Dick: I knew we would sail if we got some wind…

Dorothea: Yes, but where are we?

Dick: Lie as flat as you can. I don't believe John's sledge ever went faster. Just listen to it!

Dorothea: We're going too fast!

Dick: What!?

Dorothea: Too fast!! A thousand miles an hour!!

Dick: Probably thirty.

Dick takes his glasses off and starts wiping them

Dorothea: Don't let go!!

Dick: All right. (*He puts his glasses back on and grabs tight hold)*

Dorothea: Where are we going?

Dick: Straight up the lake. Hills on both sides, it's like a giant peashooter. And we're the pea!

Dorothea: Where are we now?

Dick: Arctic!

Dorothea: Arctic!? (*She shakes Dick's shoulder*) Let's stop! Now! At once!

Dick: We can't go back! We can't help but arrive somewhere if we keep going…

Dorothea: But where? Dick, watch out! DICK!

Blackout and a loud sound of crashing, smashing and general chaos! Then silence…sledge is struck, exit Dick and Dot.

SCENE 6 – COUNCIL AT THE FRAM (PART 2)

Peggy, John, Susan, Titty, Roger and Captain Flint "in the Fram", doors open to show they are inside.
Lighting and sound effects to show they are snug in the cabin and the blizzard rages outside.

Captain Flint: (*pacing*) This is a blizzard. Or something very like one. At least it came before Nancy set off. She's got sense enough not to start in weather like this. Anyway, her mother wouldn't let her.

Titty: No council!

Roger: No feast!

Captain Flint: Oh we'll have the feast all right. We can have another one with Nancy. No point in letting the food go to waste. But this doesn't look like stopping any time soon, so Nancy's best off where she is.

Roger: (*looking out of the window*) I can't see anything. It's worse than fog!

Susan: I'd better light the lantern.

Susan lights the lantern – moves right, Roger sits.

Captain Flint: (*pacing*) I do hope those two have the sense to keep under cover. Nancy will be all right at Beckfoot. But I'm bothered about those two. It's been snowing like this a good long time already and doesn't show any signs of stopping. The roads will be choked before very long and nobody will be going anywhere...

Titty: They're very good at thinking of things...

Captain Flint: (*softens*) Well let's hope they thought of staying indoors. Where do they go to see your signal?

John: The barn above Dixon's Farm. Near the tarn.

Captain Flint: Can they see Beckfoot promontory from up there? Might they have seen Nancy's flag?

John: Easily, yes. Dick always uses a telescope.

Captain Flint: I bet that's what's happened. They'll have seen Nancy's joy signal and gone straight across there to see what she wanted.

Titty: It's just what they would do.

Captain Flint: (*to Peggy*) Your mother wouldn't have been too pleased, but she could have them running about the garden until all the disinfecting was done.

Peggy: Nancy would have been bursting to talk to them.

Captain Flint: (*relieved – sits*) That's what's happened. They're all right, sitting at Beckfoot with Nancy trying to get a word in once every ten minutes. Well, we won't see any of them until this storm is over, so we might as well get on with the banquet. We can't starve even for their sakes.

Susan goes round with tray

Captain Flint: It's going to be quite dark before this stops. When it finally does, I'll walk with you back to Holly Howe, just to make sure you can get up the field through the drifts. Then I'll go straight up to Beckfoot, comfort poor Nancy and bring those two back.

Blackout. All exit after setting up NP

SCENE 7 – FINDING POLE / AT THE POLE

Back on a clear stage with the Ds' sledge in the middle of the stage, mast and sail off and some way away. Dick and Dorothea both lying down apart. Still effects to show heavy blowing snow.

Dick struggles to his feet.

Dick: Dot! Dot!

Dorothea also stands but starts staggering in the wrong

direction…

Dorothea: Dick?

Dick: Stand still. (*he flounders in her direction*). Hi Dot.

They hang on to each other for a minute, relieved not to be alone.

Dorothea: Are you all right? (*starts laughing nervously*)

Dick: Dot! You aren't crying?

Dorothea: It's mostly snow… But I didn't know what happened to you when the mast broke…

Dick: The mast broke?

Dorothea: Yes, it's here. Or at least it was…

Dick: The sledge is here too. Quick let's get it before we lose them both under the snow…

They collect the sledge and mast and sail and start pulling the ropes again.

Dorothea: What are we going to do?

Dick: I suppose we must be right at the head of the lake. The others might be very close by. Peggy said the North Pole was near the shore…

Dorothea: I wish Peggy was here.

Dick: She wouldn't know any better than us where to go in this weather.

Dorothea: Well we're going to have to go somewhere. It's getting worse and worse!

Dick: I know. I'll use the rope. You hold onto the other end, and I'll explore as far as it will let me. Give it a jerk and I'll jerk back. Don't jerk too hard, it's not very strong for an Alpine rope...

Dorothea: Don't go and let go of it.

Dick: I won't.

Dick walks off with the rope. ?Dry ice to give bad visibility? Dot left on her own for a couple of minutes

Dorothea: Dick!?

Dick reappears quickly

Dick: There's a house. I could just see it. Come on...

They walk off towards the windows. The dry ice starts to clear and they see it.

Dick: Here it is. It's a queer kind of a house... There must be a door somewhere...

He feels along the window. Suddenly opens them

Dick: Here, Dot! Come in.

There is a huge sign saying NORTH POLE

Dorothea: I wonder whether we're close to the North Pole?

Dick: I don't know...

Dorothea: This is a funny sort of a place. Just one room and all windows. Must be a sort of a summer house...

Dick: Look at that packing case. It looks like the one Captain Flint had...

Dorothea: (*reading*) North Polar Expedition. Ss As and Ds... To be opened by the first to reach the Pole.

Dick: The North Pole must be somewhere nearby...

Dorothea: Why haven't they opened it? Unless... unless

we're the first to reach the North Pole!

Dick looks up at the sign, looks away again. Then looks up and actually reads it.

Dick: Dot! Look! This is it! This is the place they meant! This is the Pole itself!

Dorothea: But where are the others?

Dick: We must have sailed past them. Perhaps they went for shelter when the storm hit?

Dorothea: You're right. Susan will have got them off the ice and into shelter as soon as they saw the snow coming; she wouldn't have wanted Titty and Roger out in that. They'll come along as soon as it stops. Let's get things ready, and hoist a flag.

Dick: All right. As soon as the snow stops we can signal again. Morse code this time. N. P. for North Pole. To help them find us in the dark.

Dorothea: Good idea, Dick.

Blackout – Dick and Dot stay on stage and start to signal with torches.

SCENE 8 – NANCY SEES A SIGNAL

Nancy and Mrs Blackett are outside Beckfoot.

Mrs Blackett: Are you sure you don't just want to get straight to bed?

Nancy: I've spent enough time in bed to last me the rest of the year! I'll just have a short walk to the lakeshore and back...

Mrs Blackett: It's such a shame you couldn't get together with the others today, but it just can't be helped. It's years since I've seen snow like that. Thank heavens it's stopped.

Enter Captain Flint stage left

Captain Flint: What have you done with those Ds?

Nancy: I haven't seen them!

Captain Flint: Oh where have they got to?

Mrs Blackett: Are they missing? In that blizzard?

Captain Flint: For the moment. (*Starts to leave again*). Can you rustle up the police, Molly?

Mrs Blackett: I can run up the road and see if Sammy's in...

Captain Flint: Good. I'm sure they'll turn up.

Exit Mrs Blackett and Captain Flint in opposite directions. Nancy walks to the front of the stage.

A light on the balcony starts flashing (Morse code for N.P.)

Nancy: (*to herself*) What's that light? There's nothing there, except… It's morse code. N.P. North Pole. (*running back to the house*) Mother! Mother!

Cook: (*off stage*) Your mother's gone to the Lewthwaites' to find Sammy…

Nancy: When she comes back tell them I've found them. They're at the North Pole. Uncle Jim knows where. And tell her I'm there too…

Cook: (*off stage*) But Miss Nancy!!

Nancy exits

SCENE 9 - SEARCH PARTY

Susan, Titty, Roger and Peggy are outside Holly Howe

Susan: I thought it would never stop!

Peggy: Uncle Jim was in an awful rush… I think he was still worried about Dick and Dot.

Roger: Where is John?

Susan: Well… He took the lantern and went up to the igloo. Just to check they weren't there…

Titty: Without us?

Roger: What a cheek!

Susan: It's bad enough that he's had to go up there at all, without you two coming along. Look how deep it is here!

It will be much worse up there.

Peggy: He's been gone a good long time now. I hope he's all right.

Roger: But I thought Dick and Dorothea were at Beckfoot?

Susan: Well, we hope they are, obviously...

Enter John with lantern, in a rush

John: Quick! Susan, we need to get going straight away...

Susan: Why? What's happened.

John: They weren't at the igloo. But I thought I might try up at the barn. It was a job getting there. They weren't there either, but I could see their signal...

Peggy: What?

John: North Pole. They've gone there!

Titty: But it said "Come to the *Fram*" this morning.
I wonder when they changed it?

Enter Mrs Jackson

Mrs Jackson: What's ado?

John: It's Dick and Dorothea! They were out in the blizzard. They've gone to... Peggy knows where they've gone... Come on, Susan, Peggy, we must go after them at once.

Mrs Jackson: Now, I don't know...

John: Please, tell Captain Flint... Mr Turner I mean... When he comes back. Tell him they started for the north by themselves and that we've gone to the rescue... Come on, Peggy, you know the place.

OTLEY – WINTER HOLIDAY

Peggy and Susan put their rucksacks on

Susan: If they got caught in the blizzard, anything might have happened.

Mrs Jackson: (*uncertainly*) Now you won't go too far… You won't be long.

Peggy: If Uncle Jim comes back here. Tell him North Pole. He'll understand.

Roger: But what are you going to do?

John: Relief expedition. All right Susan, Peggy. We'll have to travel on the lake because the roads are awful with snow…

Roger: But… what about us…

Susan: Bed!

John, Susan and Peggy exit.

Roger: It's not fair!

Titty: Our things are all ready…

They look at each other, pick up their rucksacks, Roger takes out a torch and lights it, they exit too.

Mrs Jackson: And what about bed for you two? (*Sees there's nobody there*) Oh. And I never saw them go. Well with Miss Susan, they'll come to no harm, I suppose…

Exit Mrs Jackson.

Peggy, John and Susan walking / sliding along the ice, John holding the lantern and the other two towing the sledge. Reach front middle of the stage. Torch light appears at edge of stage. Susan turns and sees it.

RANSOME CENTRE STAGE

Susan: Bother it!

Peggy: What?

Susan: Roger's torch...

Titty: Stop! Stop!

Susan: I ought to have made them promise to go to bed and stay there...

Titty and Roger catch up with the others

Susan: What are you two doing here? Go back, immediately!

Roger: It isn't fair!

Titty: You said yourself that anything may have happened. You may want all of us to help...

John: Let's not waste time!

Susan: We can't really send them back on their own... I don't know what Mother would say!

Titty: But the Ds are lost! They've got to be found. Daddy always says that if it's a matter of life and death, no rules count...

John: Come on. Peggy's turn with the lantern.

Susan shakes her head, crossly, but they keep going. Lighting change.

Some music and movement to show passing of time and distance up the lake.

Susan: I wonder how far they got before the snow came?

John: We may find them any minute. They'll have got off the ice the minute the storm hit.

Susan: If only they had any sense. But they haven't – not that sort of sense. People oughtn't to be allowed to be brought up in towns!

Peggy: Let's work a bit closer to the shore.

Roger: (*ghostly echoing*) Hoooo! Hoooo!

Titty: It's very lonely out here on the ice. But it must be much worse for the Ds...

Roger: (*cheerfully*) They may have starved to death. They never remember to have enough chocolate.

Peggy: What rot!

John: You've had your chocolate ration for the day, anyway...

Roger: What about the night?

All laugh.

Titty: They'll know it's us coming when they see the lantern.

Peggy: Unless they're hopeless galoots.

Peggy points over the auditorium – all stop.

Peggy: Beckfoot. I wonder why they didn't go straight there when the storm hit?

John: They didn't know Nancy was free from mumps.

Peggy: Do you think we ought to go and get Nancy? She'll be awfully sick that she missed out when she hears about this...

John: We could do...

Susan: She's probably in bed. She's been ill! Nobody

would let her out at night...

John: True.

They trudge on a little further

John: I can't believe they could have got as far as this before the blizzard hit.

Titty: They can skate awfully fast.

Peggy: They can't have been such galoots as to carry on in the blizzard!

Susan: They couldn't see where they were going.

John: How far is it to the head of the lake?

Peggy: A bit further yet.

Susan: The snow's getting deeper. It all got blown up here by the gale.

They start trudging rather than sliding.

Peggy: Oh I recognise that headland. Don't worry me hearties, we're nearly at the head of the lake now. If it were light we could see the Pole itself.

John: We'll just have to start working down the other shore, I suppose.

Peggy: We'll have to be careful where the river flows in. Over there (*she points to her left*) Captain Flint says it never freezes properly there.

John: What?

Peggy: Bad ice...

They all look at each other

Roger: What if…

Blackout. Exit right

SCENE 10 – NANCY, THEN OTHERS, REACH THE POLE

At the North Pole. Dick hangs up the lantern. Dorothea stops setting up food.

Dorothea: Dick, let's put everything back. We've got to set off back. It stopped snowing ages ago, and I'm sure they'd be here by now if they were coming…

Dick: But we can't leave now that we've signalled…

Dorothea: Oh, I don't know what to do… What will Mrs Dixon think? And Mr Dixon and Silas. They won't know where we are?

Dick: But somebody might have seen the signal and be coming. Anyway, I'm very tired.

Dorothea nods and sits down. Dick sits down too. They start to nod off.

The sound of a snowball hitting the outside of the windows.

Nancy: (*off stage*) Ahoy!

Dick and Dorothea both stir a little but don't get up.

Nancy: (*off stage*) Ahoy!!

Dorothea gets up.

Dorothea: Here they are! Get up, Dick, get up!

Dick: (*after struggling up*) Make straight for the door. It's very deep there, but it's all right now...

Nancy: (*off stage*) It's quite deep enough here! I've been fighting through it for ages.

Enter Nancy.

Dorothea: Hi Nancy! Good good. Where are the others? They haven't turned back?

Nancy: What others? I came as soon as I saw your signals. The others are at Holly Howe. But why are you here at all? Everything's fixed now. We're coming tomorrow.

Dick: (*startled*) But you put up your signal...

Nancy: What signal?

Dick: Flag at Beckfoot...

Nancy: Oh that. That was to say I could come to the council in the *Fram*. (*Dick starts flicking through his pocketbook*) The blizzard scuppered that, of course. The others were there all right and everything's settled. But you're here already!

Dick: But look. (*he shows her the page in his pocketbook*).

Nancy: (*reading*) "Flag at Beckfoot = start for pole".

Dick: I wrote it down when you told me. At the observatory when we were learning signals.

All sit

Nancy: Golly. I remember you doing it. And something happened and I never told the others. And then came mumps and I forgot every little bit about it… And then Captain Flint asked if I could put a big red flag on the flagstaff if I could come to the *Fram*… It was a bedspread…

Dick: I saw it at once. We were already late so thought the others must have already started.

Nancy: And you came here all by yourselves? Through that blizzard? How did you find the Pole?

Dorothea: The blizzard helped really.

Dick: We were sailing! (*stand*)

Nancy: (*stand*) Jib-booms and bobstays! Sailing! In that?

Dick: The wind was just right. It took us straight here.

Nancy: Well, that's the best thing I've ever heard. What a pity you did it a day early…

Dorothea: And we've gone and opened the stores. And eaten some of them, because we lost our food when we capsized…

Nancy: Capsized?!

Dick: The mast broke

Nancy: You lucky, lucky beasts. Of course you were right to open the stores. Actually, I'm starving myself. Shall we have supper? Shiver my timbers, the others will be jolly sick at missing this.

John, Peggy, Susan, Roger & Titty (*offstage*) Hurrah!!!

Nancy: What on earth? (*She stands up and walks towards the "door"*)

Enter John, Peggy, Susan, Roger & Titty

Titty: It's Nancy!

John: But Captain Flint said you were at Beckfoot.

Nancy: So I was, until I saw their lantern signals. Proper ones this time. Morse code.

John: We never saw them.

Susan: But why are they here at all?

Peggy: Why didn't they come to the council?

Nancy: It's not their fault at all. It's mine really. I told Dick a flag at Beckfoot meant "start for the Pole" and then I forgot all about it, what with mumps and everything.

John: That's all right. I thought they couldn't have done it on purpose.

Susan: At least everybody's all right. But I don't know how on earth we can all get enough rest to do it again tomorrow.

Nancy: That's the best of it! Now you're here, there's no need to do it again. We've done it! We're here! This is miles better than anything we planned. Sailing to the North Pole in a gale and a snowstorm...

John: Sailing?

Nancy: Rather. And nobody knowing where anybody else was... Tomorrow was going to be just be like a picnic. This was much better. Everybody's done very well.

Roger: (*walking over to the food*) Including Captain Flint... (*he picks up some snack or other and starts eating*)

Susan: Well we shall have to stay the night now. I'm sure Mother would say it was the right thing to do. The main thing is that we're all here.

There is music while they quickly all nod off

SCENE 11 – THE POLE

Enter Captain Flint and Mrs Blackett. They creep in, Mrs Blackett counting heads quickly. Dorothea sits up, sleepily.

Dorothea: Sh!

Mrs Blackett: Sh!

Dorothea falls back asleep. Captain Flint mimes building the fire up and then he and Mrs Blackett find somewhere to sleep too and both drop off.

Lights slowly build to show dawn. Susan wakes first, and then Dorothea

Susan: Sh! (*she points at Captain Flint and Mrs Blackett, fast asleep*)

Nancy also wakes up.

Dorothea: (*to Nancy*) Sh!

Nancy: Giminy. Well done mother!

Roger: (*loudly*) What time is it?

Everybody else wakes. Roger, Titty, Peggy, Dick and John, all surprised to see Captain Flint and Mrs Blackett.

Mrs Blackett: Well Nancy, you dreadful girl. And you

Peggy. And I've been telling everybody how sensible Susan is... and I don't doubt that if the truth were known it would turn out to be your Uncle Jim's fault as much as anybody's...

Captain Flint: Oh Molly, I was just a beast of burden! Anyway, if all had gone to plan we were going to come up the lake today, have a feast and return this evening. What could be more harmless than that?

Nancy: Or more dull?! This was much better. And anyway, mother, you wouldn't have come to the North Pole in the middle of the night. And you wouldn't have missed that for the world!

Mrs Blackett: Wouldn't I?

Captain Flint: We would have been here sooner, but we had to race around and call off the search parties...

Big reaction

Nancy: Real ones?

Captain Flint: Yes. Hard to believe people would go off in search of a bunch of worthless children instead of getting their night's rest...

Susan: Do you take sugar in your tea, Mrs Blackett?

Mrs Blackett: Two lumps please, Susan.

Captain Flint: Ha, polar hospitality!

Peggy: Shiver my timbers! Things couldn't have worked out better.

Nancy: (*stay put*) Who taught you to shiver timbers?

Peggy: Just while you were away...

Nancy: Did you use any of my other words?

Peggy: Some of them

Nancy: Jib-booms and bobstays?

Peggy: Yes

Nancy: Barbecued billygoats?

Peggy: Yes

Roger: She even called people galoots!

Nancy: Well I bet it all helped.

Captain Flint: Going by results… I'd say it did.

Titty: Well, we made it to the North Pole. Shall we go out and have a snowball fight?

Nancy: Why not?

Finish with a big snowball fight involving everybody (including audience). Song: We Set Sail, opportunities for bows for everybody (including two/three cast members not initially involved in the snowball fight).

THE END

and finally, an authentic script dating from well before TARS ....

EVGENIA'S *SWALLOWS AND AMAZONS*

The Twilight Years – Hill Top (Amazon Publications, 2017) sets out in full the 'Affair' the sorry tale of the BBC 1962 production of *Swallows & Amazons*, a six part serial.

'Sorry' because no element of it (apart from the money) satisfied either Arthur or Evgenia. Right from the start, they both wanted the script to follow the book exactly – as all authors do!

Several script writers were drafted in. None met with approval. Evgenia was desperate to preserve the integrity of Arthur's work and finally wrote a script herself which was forwarded to the script writer. (Appendix IV in *The Twilight Years*)

How exactly was this followed in the finished version of the film? How far exactly did it follow the dialogue in the book? Was it used at all?

Since it is an absolutely authentic scripted version of S & A, it is definitely appropriate to include it in this selection.

Margaret Ratcliffe

****

Evgenia's script

[the numbers which appear at intervals in the script below may refer to scenes and sequences in the original script.]

3248 116.

EXT. LOOK-OUT POINT. EARLY MORNING

Dead calm. Rather misty. The children arrive carrying a coil of rope and the hurricane lantern.

John "When the mist clears there will be some wind, I hope."

John ties one end of the rope round his waist and swarms up the tall pine tree. Susan pays out the rope and watches that it does not catch on anything.

John sits astride the thick lowest branch with his back against the trunk. He unties the rope from his waist and starts coiling it. When he thinks he's got enough he drops down his coil so that the rope hangs over the branch with both ends touching the ground.

John "Hang on to both ends and keep them away from the tree while I come down."

On the ground he ties one end of the rope to the handle of the lantern and the other round the oil reservoir. He hauls it up and down a few times. He unties the lantern, joins the two ends of the rope and ties this doubled end round the tree.

John "Now we are ready to sail at night."

117.

To careen means to turn the boat over on to her side for scrubbing, painting or repairing the part which is under water while she is afloat. If the boat is already overturned why do they want to careen her? Why do they want the boat to lie on her side at this particular moment? If you merely want to provide work for idle hands – there are a number of little jobs they can usefully do while waiting.

Nancy "The secret is to lure them here …"

But there is no need to "lure" them. It is made very clear that if the wind is from the south (as it is this day) it would make it easier for the Swallows to sail to the Amazon River and try to capture the Amazon. Therefore Nancy and Peggy know that the Swallows will be coming. According to the actual location at the time of filming it may be misleading to mention the points of the compass here and probably impossible to show in mime the direction at the wind and in which party's favour it works.

EVGENIA'S *SWALLOWS AND AMAZONS*

I think Nancy should say

Nancy "The wind is fair for the Swallows. All we have to do when they come is to keep out of sight. But as soon as they come we shall quietly slip away, sail for the island and land."

LOOK-OUT POINT MORNING

John "Look! The mist is nearly gone. And the wind couldn't be fairer."

Susan "So what are the plans for to-day?"

John *(solemnly quoting from one of his father's books)*

"In Naval warfare two things are important; to know exactly what you want to do, and to do it in the manner that your enemy least expects."

Titty "What do the Amazons expect?"

John " With this wind they expect us to try to cut out their boat and to do it early enough to get back here in daylight."

Susan "Yes. Of course."

John "But we won't. Not until dark. We shall sail now as far as the islands off Rio and there keep a look-out to see if the Amazon leaves the Amazon River. If we don't see her by dusk it must mean that they think we have given up. They don't know about our lights. We then sail into their river, find the boathouse, pinch their boat and sail both boats back here."

Titty "A jolly good plan!"

John "But it means that somebody will have to stay on the island to light the lanterns."

Titty "I'll stay."

John "I am afraid it will have to be you. Susan will be wanted to sail our prize and I don't think Roger can manage it."

Susan "Titty, are you sure you don't mind?"

Titty "Of course not. I'd love to stay."

John "You light and hoist the lighthouse lantern as soon as it begins to get dark. But the candles in the small lanterns won't last long so you must light them only when you are sure that we are coming. We shall give you three owl hoots to let you know."

Titty "Aye aye, Sir."

3245

176. Cont.

Titty "We've found it! We've found it!"

Roger "Wouldn't Capt. Flint be glad?"

Titty "We must go and tell him. But we must first go and tell John and Susan. I do hope they are still asleep and don't know yet that we have marooned them."

They get into the boat and row as fast as they can towards Wild Cat

EXT. HOUSEBOAT. STILL QUITE EARLY MORNING

All the Swallows in their boat approach the houseboat rowing. Capt. Flint appears on the after-deck yawning. The Swallows shout all together "Good Morning"

Capt. Flint "Good morning. What brings you out so early? Nothing's wrong I hope."

Titty "We've found your treasure."

EVGENIA'S *SWALLOWS AND AMAZONS*

Capt. Flint "You haven't really found anything, have you?"

Titty "Yes, we have. Come and we'll show you."

Capt. Flint "I think we'll all go in my boat, more room. Just get your painter round that cleat in the stem."

They all get into Capt. Flint's large rowing boat, Capt. Flint taking one pair of oars, John the other. They row away fast, towing the Swallow.

ON CORMORANT ISLAND. MORNING.

Capt. Flint kneels by the hole where the trunk is. The children stand round him.

Capt. Flint "You are right. This is my seaman's chest. Well done Titty!"

He pulls out a bunch of keys from his pocket, unlocks the box and lifts the lid revealing a lot of diaries, log books, a small typewriter in its case and a great bundle of typewritten paper

3244

Roger (*looking disappointed*) "Titty said treasure. But it's only books and paper and things."

Capt. Flint "There is treasure and treasure. You know, Titty, I can never thank you enough for finding mine."

Titty "The pirates said they were coming for it that is why I wanted to look for it today. Tomorrow would have been probably too late."

Capt. Flint (*looking at his watch*) "I am sorry but I must go now. In a few minutes someone will be waiting for me on shore by the houseboat."

RANSOME CENTRE STAGE

Roger *(eagerly)* "Another pirate to stay with you?"

Capt. Flint "No. Only a boy from the shop to deliver a parcel."

Susan "And we must hurry to the camp. We haven't had our breakfast yet."

Capt. Flint lifts the box on his shoulder and carries it to his boat and very carefully lowers it in. He gets into his boat, the children into theirs and they row away.

Capt. Flint "Don't forget, 3 o'clock'"

3241/42/49/50 177.

EXT. HOUSEBOAT BAY. AFTERNOON. SUNNY AND VERY HOT

The houseboat is moored as usual to her barrel buoy. A very large green flag with a large white elephant on it flies from her short flagstaff.

Captain Flint, dressed in a white shirt and slacks with a red handkerchief round his middle for a belt, bo'sn's whistle on a lanyard round his neck and a white sun helmet on his head is busy on the foredeck getting the cannon ready to fire.

The Swallow and the Amazon appear at the mouth of the bay sailing close enough to each other to talk.

John "Lower the sails as we come alongside. Swallow on port side, Amazon on starboard. Grapple and board him. Blow your whistle Mr. Mate!"

Capt. Flint fires the cannon. A loud bang.
For a while there is nothing to see but smoke. Capt. Flint blows his whistle Susan hers, the din is deafening.
When the smoke clears the small boats are much nearer to the houseboat. Susan, out of breath, hands the whistle to Roger.

EVGENIA'S *SWALLOWS AND AMAZONS*

Susan "You blow now."

Capt. Flint fires again. When the smoke clears it is seen that the little boats are very close to the houseboat.

Capt. Flint's next shot follows almost immediately after the last. Through the smoke John's voice is heard.

John "Board now! Down with the elephant!"

When it is possible to see again the small boats are alongside the houseboat, their sails are down. John is tying Swallow's painter to the rail round the after deck. He swings on board by the rail, steps over it and turns round to give a hand to Susan who is climbing after him.

Roaring "Death or Glory" Capt. Flint comes on deck by the companion steps with a large scarlet cushion in each hand, swipes at John with one of them and brings him down on deck. John jumps up quickly and charges head down into Capt. Flint. Susan pulls a cushion out of Capt. Flint's hand and gives him a mighty blow with it. Titty and Roger fasten their arms round Capt. Flint's legs, one round each leg, and cling rather like terriers.

Nancy and Peggy scramble on board by the foredeck. They run over the cabin roof yelling wildly. Nancy jumps from the roof on to Capt. Flint's back and nearly strangles him clasping her arms round his neck. Overwhelmed by numbers he comes down heavily on deck. His sun helmet rolls off.

Nancy "Yield! Yield!!"

Capt. Flint "Not while my flag is flying. Elephant for ever!"

Titty runs forward and hauls down the Elephant flag.

John "We've won. Your flag is struck."

RANSOME CENTRE STAGE

Capt. Flint *(struggling to a sitting position)* "Why, so it is. Quick work. I surrender."

Nancy "Bind him."

A coil of rope is lying handy. John and Peggy tie his legs together. They then wind the rope round and round to fasten his arms to his body.

Titty, *having walked all round the decks,* "If we are going to make him walk the plank there is one already on the foredeck."

Nancy "And so there is. But how are we going to get him there?"

Peggy "Untie his legs and let him walk over the cabin roof."

Capt. Flint "It won't bear my weight."

In the end they untie his legs and make a kind of leading string out of this end of the rope. They help him to get on his feet and make him walk along the extremely narrow gangway to the foredeck, Nancy pulling him by the leading string and John walking behind him ready to pull or to push if necessary. The others run over the cabin roof Roger being the last. He picks up the sun helmet and arrives on the foredeck carrying it in his hand.

Nancy *(letting go of the leading string)* "Tie the prisoner to the mast."

John and Peggy tie Capt. Flint to the flagstaff. Roger puts the sun helmet on, it is so much too big for him that it covers his ears and most of his face. Capt. Flint laughs.

Capt. Flint "Do you mind getting this pirate out of my sun helmet and putting it on my own head. A last wish, you know."

EVGENIA'S *SWALLOWS AND AMAZONS*

Susan takes the helmet off Roger's head and puts it on Capt. Flint's.

Nancy "Now hands up all who are for making him walk the plank."

All hands go up except John's and Susan's.

Nancy "Oh, look here! No weakening now!"

John "I think we ought to untie his hands and give him a chance to swim for it."

Nancy "Do we all agree to that?"

All hands go up.

Nancy "Bandage his eyes and get him onto the plank."

Peggy bandages his eyes with her handkerchief. John and Susan take him by the arms and guide him to the plank with Titty and Roger pushing him from behind.

Nancy *(very loud and fierce)* "Now, walk!"

Capt. Flint moves his feet very slowly and carefully along the plank until he is very near the end.

Capt. Flint "Mercy! Mercy!"

Nancy *(stamping her foot)* "WALK, or …. !"

Capt. Flint takes a deep breath, takes a step forward, falls in with a tremendous splash and goes under, his helmet stays bobbing on the ripples. He stays under rather a long time. Titty gets worried.

Titty "Perhaps he can't swim? I never thought of it."

Capt. Flint comes to the surface blowing, spluttering and tearing the bandage from his eyes and sinks again. Then he comes up this time close to the floating sun helmet, he picks it up and throws it on board the houseboat. Suddenly he lets out a fearful yell.

Capt. Flint "Sharks! Sharks! The place is stiff with them!"

Roger *(hopefully)* "Are there really sharks here?"

Capt. Flint "A rope! A rope! Throw me a rope!"

Susan *(to Nancy)* "Let's give him a rope. He has been a good long time in the water."

Nancy *(to Susan)* "All right." *(to Capt. Flint)* "We'll give you a rope."

Capt. Flint "I'd much rather a rope ladder. There is one by the spring board, I mean the plank of course. It is made fast. Just throw over the loose end."

John throws the rope ladder overboard. Capt. Flint climbs up and stands on deck swinging his arms about his chest. The water streaming off him.

Capt. Flint "What are you going to do with me now? Do you think my crimes are wiped out? Because if they are…"

Swallows and Amazons *together* "WHAT?"

Capt. Flint "All the best sea fights end with a banquet. There is one waiting in the cabin. Just let me change into something dry and …"

Capt. Flint lowers himself down the fore-hatch. A moment later he puts his head out.

Capt. Flint "By the way, I suppose you'll want to hoist the Jolly Roger on your prize. You will find one in the locker."

EVGENIA'S *SWALLOWS AND AMAZONS*

Peggy gets it from the locker, takes elephant flag off halyard.

3238/39/40

184. Cont.

Capt. Flint lifts the paper cover and discloses a large cake decorated with very wavy icing and two little sailing boats also made from icing.

Roger "The SWALLOW and the AMAZON!"

Capt. Flint "That is what they are meant to be."

Nancy suddenly very sorry for herself.

Nancy (*to Capt. Flint*) "It is jolly unfair! Schools and lessons for us, junketing and enjoying yourself all the winter in Africa for you."

Capt. Flint "Not enjoying myself. Doing quite a hard job."

Titty "I wish I was going to Africa. I'd love to see forests full of parrots."

Capt. Flint "I shall bring back a parrot for you. It's the least I can do to show my gratitude. Which kind do you like?

Titty "I like the green ones best."

Capt. Flint "I may as well bring back parrots all round if you want them."

Roger "I don't want a parrot. Can you bring me a monkey, please?"

Capt. Flint "With or without a tail?"

Roger "With a tail, please. The others are only apes."

Susan (*very sternly to Roger*) "You must first ask mother if she minds."

Roger "She won't mind if it is a very little one."

John "It has been a lovely holiday."

Nancy "But much too short."

Capt. Flint "Cheer up! You are coming again next year. Aren't you?

Titty "Next year and every year for ever and ever."

They have been eating steadily all the time and there is hardly any food left on the table.

Peggy *(rising)* "It is getting rather stuffy in the cabin. Let's go and sit on deck. Uncle Jim do play your accordion."

Capt. Flint goes into fo'c'sle and comes back with the accordion.

Capt. Flint "Luckily the burglars did not think fo'c'sle worth burgling or they'd have taken it for certain.

They all rise and shout "Thank you" "Thank you very much"

Titty "Good bye Polly. See you again next year. Say 'Pieces of eight' say it just once. 'Pieces of eight!' "

Parrot "Pieces of eight!"

Everybody stops in surprise and looks at the parrot.

Nancy "Shiver my timbers! He never said it for us!"

Capt. Flint "I say, Titty. It is a long time to wait till I come back in the spring. Would you like to have Polly now? You said you liked them green."

Titty can hardly believe her ears. She stammers in her surprise and happiness.

EVGENIA'S *SWALLOWS AND AMAZONS*

Titty "Am I, am I really to take it?"

Capt. Flint "Of course you are. You've earned it about ten thousand times."

Titty "Thank you. Thank you so much."

Roger *(sadly)* "My monkey will come next year."

Capt. Flint "If your mother says you may have it, I'll see about it at once. There are monkeys nearer than Africa. You might get your monkey next week."

Roger *(cheering up)* "I'll ask her as soon as we get home tonight."

Titty "Capt. Flint, won't you be lonely without Polly?"

Capt. Flint "I must think of him too. He is a young parrot and I am a dull companion for him. It is much better for him to be with young people like yourself."

They all go on deck through the companion way. They sing to the accordion for a while.

185. 186. 187. 188. 189 could not be tightened and sharpened without knowing the actual location.

25

[The following note is in Evgenia' handwriting and is slightly different from the typed version above.]

117.

To careen means to turn the boat on her side for scrubbing, repairing or painting the part of the boat which is under water when she is afloat. So why careen the already overturned boat? Why should the Amazons want to careen their boat at this particular moment?

Physically it would be impossible for them to do it inside their boathouse. If you merely want to provide work for the idle hands – there are plenty of little jobs they can do instead.
Nancy "The secret is to lure ??? over here" ... But there is no need "to lure" them. It is made clear in the book that the wind from the south would make it easier for the Swallows to sail to the Amazon river and try to capture the Amazon. Therefore Nancy and Peggy know that the Swallows will be coming as the wind is south. According to the actual location where the film will be taken it may be misleading to mention the points of the compass and it may be impossible to show silently the direction of the wind and in which party's favour it works. So, I think, Nancy should say

Nancy "The wind is fair for them. All we have to do when they come is to keep out of sight. They will think we are hiding somewhere here with our boat. But as soon as it is safe we shall sail to the island, I shall land and hide there."

If you could make it clearer and simpler – please do.

Arthur and Evgenia at Hill Top.

RANSOME CENTRE STAGE

Epilogue

Well! What Talented Tars we have!

Gathered together as a collection, we can only marvel at the dedication and ingenuity of our contributors.

What variety! And all based on Arthur Ransome and his Works.

What authenticity! Both Arthur and Evgenia, who set such store by the original works, would unquestionably approve wholeheartedly of these diverse dramatic offerings.

Surely, surely we must hope some or all of them will be revived; either by TARS at events or perhaps external troupes, amateur or professional, might be interested. A musical evening perhaps, round a campfire or enlivening an IAGM or Literary Weekend.

We are so pleased to have enabled this unique collection of dramatic works. Performance rights are reserved, but both the publishers and, we are sure, the individual authors, would be delighted to give permission for future productions. However, such permission must be sought of the publishers in the first instance.

Attentive readers of the list of subscribers may suspect that not all are current members. However, all are known to Brian Hopton, and he has ensured they are fully paid up.

Acknowledgements

First and foremost, our thanks are due to the **authors** of our plays, together with their **cast members** who put a lot of work into their parts. None of the plays would have happened without team effort, and now they have ransacked old cupboards to find these historic documents.

Next, I have to thank the people who have given me enormous assistance towards the actual preparation of the book.

Jill Goulder and **Paul Crisp** were very active in Brian Hopton's plays, and without their memories of them a lot would have been lost.

Kirstie Taylor is another Tar who remembers what actually went on in those early years of the society, now almost lost in the mists of time.

Diana Sparkes has kept records of her parts in Brian's plays.

Margaret Ratcliffe and her husband **Joe** have, as always, been a strong support throughout, even when touring Spain in a motorhome, and at the mercy of doubtful Internet connections. And above all, they have designed the cover, very much in the spirit of "the twelve".

Brian Hopton's stenographer, **Miss Margaret Turner**, not quite the Great-Aunt and not at all alarming, converted all his vital texts into documents that my computer could read, unlike Brian's handwriting. That has saved me many hours of frustrating work.

And we have to thank **Stephen Sykes** of Hill Top for suggesting we present Evgenia's attempts to improve on the BBC to a wider audience.

Photograph credits

In the Brian Hopton section, all are by him and the late Tony Parslow. Kirstie Taylor has supplied those of the Scottish Smolny duologue and *Bohemia in Durham*. And the AusTars pictures are from Jan Allen. Duncan Hall found us an original poster for the Otley *Winter Holiday*.

For the photo of Arthur and Evgenia at Hill Top, we have to thank the Brotherton Library and Ransome's Literary Executors.

Cover illustration:
Proscenium Arch, Metropolitan Opera House, Philadelphia, from *The Victrola Book of the Opera*, 1917 (Wikimedia Commons, Public Domain)

Amazon Publications

List of Subscribers

Stuart and Janet Allen
Charles H Ball
Prof Michael Balls
Mr H Bangate
Mrs Barrable
Rosemary Beal
Christopher Birt
Mrs Braithwaite
Sammy Braithwaite
David Branston
Nick Brewster
Rowan Brockhurst
Stephen Burrell
Andrew Caird
John C Cooper
Mrs Audrie J Cossar
Sean Croshaw
Evelyn Dagley
George Derbyshire
Mrs Dixon
Peter Edmonds
Paul Endicott
Doug Faunt
Nora C Fawcett
Kirsty N Findlay
M W P Fisher
Barbara Flower
Robert Froom
Jill Goulder
Michael Haines
David Hambleton
Dr Fiona Haughey
Ronald Hullabaloo
Robert C James
Ian R Johnson
Lt Col T E Jolys DSO
Francis Kirkland
Christopher Kirwin
Catherine Lamont
Stewart Linham
James Lonie
Bob Lowman
The McGinnis Family
Janet Mearns
David Y Middleton
Robert Milne
Peter Milroy
Joy and Graham Morrell
John Nichols
Cheryl Paget
Robin J Parker
John C Parsloe
Jonathan Pearson
Stephanie Phillips Morgan
Judith Powell
Roger Powell

RANSOME CENTRE STAGE

Susan D Price
Mary Pritchard
Ms W R Reis
Jeremy H A Roberts
Neil Robertson
Paul Rodwell
Alasdair Shaw
Andrew Silk
David W Smith
Duncan Smith
Judy Snook
Diana Sparkes
Port 'N' Starboard
Mr Timothy Stedding
Paul S Sykes
Stephen and Janine Sykes
Sayoko Tasumi
Mrs K Taylor
PC Alfred Tedder
Dave Thewlis
Miss Maria Turner
Rex Wade
Davin Wakeford
Ian Wall
Jeremy Ward
Mrs Whittle
Peter Willis
Philip Winter
The Arthur Ransome
    Society in Australia
Anonymous (3)